'A must-read book. I loved reading it. Lucy Brazier delivers a truly knowledgeable, heart-driven book for assistants and their leaders.' SAMANTHA COX, COO, CENTRAL REAL CAPITAL AND FORMER EA TO SIR RICHARD BRANSON

'Essential reading for elevating your presence and role. Pulsating with invaluable information and guidance, this book will empower you to become an indispensable force in an ever-changing landscape of the assistant role' LIBBY MOORE, FORMER CHIEF OF STAFF TO OPRAH WINFREY

'This book has the potential to change not only individual careers but entire organizations. Readers will find themselves rapidly turning the pages to digest the knowledgeable, confident and encouraging mentorship of Lucy Brazier.' ANN HIATT, LEADERSHIP STRATEGIST, FORMER EA TO JEFF BEZOS AND FORMER CHIEF OF STAFF TO ERIC SCHMIDT

'Prepare to be inspired, equipped, and motivated as you dive into the pages of *The Modern-Day Assistant*. This book will inspire you to reach new heights of excellence and become an invaluable asset to any organization.' HELEN MONUMENT, CHAIR, WORLD ADMINISTRATORS ALLIANCE

The Modern-Day Assistant

*Build your influence and
boost your potential*

Lucy Brazier

KoganPage

First published in Great Britain and the United States in 2023 by Kogan Page Limited

2nd Floor, 45 Gee Street
London
EC1V 3RS
United Kingdom
www.koganpage.com

8 W 38th Street, Suite 902
New York, NY 10018
USA

4737/23 Ansari Road
Daryaganj
New Delhi 110002
India

Kogan Page books are printed on paper from sustainable forests.

© Lucy Brazier, 2023

ISBNs
Hardback   978 1 3986 1222 8
Paperback 978 1 3986 1220 4
Ebook   978 1 3986 1221 1

British Library Cataloguing-in-Publication Data
A CIP record for this book is available from the British Library.

Library of Congress Cataloging-in-Publication Data
Names: Brazier, Lucy, author.
Title: The modern-day assistant : build your influence and boost your potential / Lucy Brazier.
Description: London, United Kingdom ; New York, NY : Kogan Page, 2023. | Includes bibliographical references and index.
Identifiers: LCCN 2023029142 (print) | LCCN 2023029143 (ebook) | ISBN 9781398612204 (paperback) | ISBN 9781398612228 (hardback) | ISBN 9781398612211 (ebook)
Subjects: LCSH: Secretaries. | Administrative assistants. | BISAC: BUSINESS & ECONOMICS / Personal Success | BUSINESS & ECONOMICS / Development / Business Development
Classification: LCC HD8039.S58 B73 2023 (print) | LCC HD8039.S58 (ebook) | DDC 650.1/4--dc23/eng/20230622
LC record available at https://lccn.loc.gov/2023029142
LC ebook record available at https://lccn.loc.gov/2023029143

Typeset by Hong Kong FIVE Workshop, Hong Kong
Print production managed by Jellyfish
Printed and bound by CPI Group (UK) Ltd, Croydon CR0 4YY

*To Marcus, Charlotte and Sam, who put the Mar, Cha &
Am in Marcham Publishing and are my reason for being.*

*To Duncan for loving me enough to let me go and fulfil my
mission to change the world for assistants.*

*And to Bob, Matthew and Fran – three of the best assistants
I could have asked for. With love and gratitude for
serving me so that I could go and serve them.*

Contents

Foreword

I met Lucy Brazier just before the Covid-19 pandemic at a conference for administrative professionals in Dubai. She was chairing the event and I was one of several guest speakers, each of us booked to share our knowledge of the multi-dimensional world of executive support. By the time the conference was over, I had joined the hundreds around the globe who look upon Lucy not just as a consummate expert in her field but also as a friend.

My knowledge of executive support – such as it was – was gained through practical experience working for Princess Diana, first as her military aide and then as Private Secretary/Chief of Staff. It was largely a process of trial and error but, thanks to my very professional and also very patient royal boss, I quickly acquired the skills required to run a busy private office as well as the small matter of organizing the public life of one of the most famous women in the world.

Like many in the executive assistant business, I had to learn fast. As a career, it was thrilling, terrifying, inspiring and always a privilege. Perhaps scariest of all, there was no instruction manual I could thumb through to find the answers to the hundreds of questions and problems that seemed to land on my desk every day. I was on my own – and failure was not an option.

How I wish I could have found a copy of Lucy's brilliant *The Modern-Day Assistant* hidden somewhere on a palace bookshelf. Because this is a truly remarkable book. At first glance, it's another of those business tomes that promises to transform your working life from drudgery to a gleaming pathway of success. And, it's true, here is a goldmine of invaluable professional advice for every executive assistant (by whatever title you know them since, as Lucy reminds us, today's EA may wear a bewildering variety of job descriptions).

Among much else, you'll find the last word on how to hone your professional network, how to manage a project and how to adapt to modern hybrid working arrangements. And then you'll learn the invisible skills of how to navigate office politics, maximize your leadership potential and master the art of emotional intelligence. Everything, in short, the 21st-century assistant might need to survive and thrive in today's ever-shifting workplace environment.

But *The Modern-Day Assistant* is far more than a dry, technical 'how to' guide. Get ready to be surprised: it's inspirational, entertaining, funny and poignant. It's a business book all right, but one that warms your heart just as much as it engages your brain. That's because Lucy crams into its pages all the know-how, wisdom, anecdotes and humour she herself has accumulated during a remarkable lifetime in which she has lived the full spectrum of office life, from the humble tasks of junior staff to the rarified heights of the CEO.

Her unique advantage is that she only writes about what she knows and, take it from me, what she knows on this subject is all you need to know to succeed as an EA. That's because she has not only talked to thousands of you, she has also been the boss who understands how much an effective EA can transform a manager's efficiency, earning ability and all-round happiness.

Here we come to perhaps the book's greatest strength: it really has something for everybody. You may be neither a modern-day assistant nor a CEO but there will still be nuggets of practical advice for you between its covers, wrapped in the kind of unobtrusive good sense you might hope to receive from an exceptionally gifted mentor.

'Build your influence and boost your potential' is the subtitle, neatly summarizing what most of us would want to achieve in our working lives – and beyond. That's why I already know that my copy will be in constant use, travelling with me on business while also enlightening me whenever I need a shot of Lucy's straight talk and practical know-how.

As I explored the manuscript for this Foreword, I realized this book can be like a good friend: telling you what you need to know without ever nagging or talking down to you. And, like a good friend, it will help pick you up when, inevitably, you have a setback. In short, *The Modern-Day Assistant* is far more than just a book: it's an assistant for an assistant and a treasure trove for managers everywhere. Don't be surprised if it becomes your colleague, adviser, companion and confidante far into the future.

Patrick Jephson
Former Private Secretary (Chief of Staff)
to Diana, Princess of Wales

Acknowledgements

Writing this book has been one of the most interesting, thrilling and challenging projects I have ever embarked upon, not least because of time limitations. A great deal of the first draft was written in hotel rooms and on planes (with a night light while the rest of the plane was in darkness).

It would never have happened without the support and encouragement of some incredible people in my life.

My family, first and foremost, are and always have been a constant source of love and encouragement. Marcus, Charlotte and Sam, Mr Brazier, Mum and Dad and my sisters Mimi and Emma. You are my heart and are my first point of reference – always.

Granny and Grandad – no longer here, but they reminded me at every opportunity that I was never to forget how much I meant to them. They were extraordinary, ordinary people who left me with a lifelong love of hard work, self-belief and a striving for excellence.

My team, who advised me that I didn't have time to write it – and you were right! Thank you for buying into the mission to support me anyway so I could get it out there. And for all your hard work every day to support assistants from all four corners of the world.

The team at Kogan Page for taking this first-timer and making me look so good. Matt James, Susi Lowndes and Emma Dodworth – you are miracle workers. Thank you for your sound advice and endless patience.

All those who made contributions to the content, those who allowed themselves to be quoted and those who provided endorsements. Thank you for taking the time to read the manuscript to make sure that I had got it absolutely right.

In the last 12 years, during my travels, I have learned from the best in all sorts of arenas, and this book is in no small part, my thoughts around what I have learned from them. Ann Hiatt, Bonnie Low-Kramen, Cathy Harris, Danielle de Wulf, Eth Lloyd, Heather Baker, Helen Clarke, Helen Monument, Jeff Hoffman, Joan Burge, Karen Nussbaum, Laura Belgrado, Laura Schwartz, Libby Moore, Melba Duncan, Reggie Love, Rhonda Scharf, Samantha Cox, Simone White, Sue France, Susie Barron-Stubley, Veronica Cochran, Zelda la Grange – thank you for your friendship and support. The profession is indebted to every one of you.

Jo Denby – I hope that the gift that you gave me in 2003, *Executive Secretary Magazine,* has in turn become a gift for the administrative professionals of the world. Thank you for trusting me with its potential.

Patrick Jephson – from the moment I met you, I knew we were on the same page. Thank you from the bottom of my heart for the very generous Foreword. I remain in awe of your ability to balance professionalism and warmth.

Those who nominated me for my OBE: I will be eternally grateful to you for giving me one of the high points of my career. My scroll, signed by the Queen, hangs proudly in my hallway.

My personal board of directors in each arena of my life, thank you for keeping me on the straight and narrow, for listening and for caring. You have been with me through all my successes but also through some truly low points. And you were still there anyway! Julie Richards, Katie Lay, Kate Taylor, Emma Reynolds, Marion Lowrence, Peggy Vasquez, Kemetia Foley, Vickie Sokol Evans, Debbi Shaffer, Nina Aunula, Bonnie Low Kramen, Eth Lloyd, Shelagh Donnelly, Kathleen Drum, Pepita Soler, Melissa Esquibel, Caitlin Limmer, Teri Wells, Paula Moio, Cathy Harris and Ann Hiatt – I don't know what I would do without you all.

Jim Hay, my first publishing director, for being the kind of publisher that I wanted to be. In the middle of the magazine publishing rat race, you showed me that I didn't need to be a rat to survive. I am proud to have become a publisher who does her best every day to be ethical and operate with integrity. I had a great role model.

All the speakers, trainers, authors, associations, networks, sponsors and experts from across the globe that I have had the privilege of working with since I launched Marcham Publishing. You are a constant source of inspiration. Thank you for so generously sharing your knowledge with the profession. It has been my honour to go on this journey with you to change the world for assistants. We are now one profession with one voice, and we are stronger for it.

Teri Wells and Anel Martin for giving me the opportunity to be a director of Isipho Admin Foundation back in 2016. It is one of the greatest joys of my life to serve this community and to be 'changing lives, one person at a time' with both you and our incredible mentors.

All the individuals who have worked for Marcham Publishing over the years. Whether we are still in contact or not, please know how much I valued your input at the time.

My three incredible assistants – Elizabeth Claridge, Matthew Want and Fran Lielje who have managed my life and left me free to go do the things I love to do. You exemplify what exceptional executive support looks like.

And of course, all of you. I have met thousands of you over the last 12 years, from all across the world. Thank you for coming to hear me speak, for booking me to teach in your organizations, for reading the magazine, for attending our conferences and for getting me in front of your HR departments to talk about the Global Skills Matrix.

Together we are changing the world for administrative professionals. There is still much work to be done, but we are getting there.

Introduction

A successful assistant in the post-pandemic world must be agile, adaptable and possess a range of interpersonal and technical skills to thrive in an ever-changing work environment.

Ultimately your success will be determined by your ability to achieve your goals, make a positive impact, and find fulfilment in your work.

For 12 years, my passion has been to help you to step into your potential, to believe in yourself as a core part of both your business's and your manager's success, to understand how to position yourself to ensure that your role is seen as a career and not a job, and how to become one of the best assistants on the planet.

I'm going to show you how to become an exceptional assistant. One who is highly valued, partners at the highest level with your manager, and is part of the core business rather than 'just support'.

I spend most of my life travelling the world and talking to thousands of assistants, presenting at events, training in businesses and talking to leadership teams about how to best utilize their assistants. I have visited over 60 countries and spoken at over 600 events.

And when I travel, I make it my business to find out what the issues are for you currently so that I can ensure that when I'm teaching, everything that you're learning is relevant and the most up-to-date thinking.

I share real-time stories from assistants that I have met all over the world and solutions that they have worked out for themselves.

The point of this book? To bring the learning to a wider audience and to ensure that every assistant can benefit from what I have learned.

But before we do that, I want to ask you four questions. This will help you understand precisely where YOU are at the beginning of this journey.

My first question is, what are your professional ambitions? Where do you see yourself in five years? Or are you so busy doing the job that you haven't ever had time to think about it? Because that's where most assistants are. They are so busy operating in crisis mode and firefighting that they don't have time to step back and think about where they want to be. We're going to talk a lot in this book about being proactive rather than reactive. How will you ever get to your destination if you don't have a map?

The second question is, what are your current boundaries and authority? What are you allowed to do? What are you not allowed to do? And if you're honest with yourself, if there are things that you would love to be able to do, is the reason you aren't doing them yet because you have never asked? Either because you're worried that they might think that you are getting above yourself, or because you know you don't want the rejection if they say no, or because you don't think they would even consider it? Whatever it is, it's a risk worth taking if it creates opportunity. You will often have a better insight into how to do things, particularly when it comes to process and procedure, so it's important that you find your voice and speak up. We'll talk more about why process and procedure are core skills in Chapter 1.

The third question is, what are your strengths and what are your weaknesses? When teaching my course live, I often start by doing that annoying thing that trainers often do. I ask you to introduce yourself, tell me your name, tell me which company you're from and tell me how long you've been an assistant. And then I ask, 'Tell me something that you're exceptional at.' And that's where it all falls apart. Because most people look at me and say, 'I don't really know'.

I want you to think about it because there will be at least one thing that you're terrific at. It's just that you're not very good at recognizing it. The former CEO of the International Association of Administrative Professionals (IAAP), Dr Veronica Cochran, raised an interesting point in her inaugural speech when she said that assistants often come from a point of limitation. They didn't decide to become an assistant; they often fell into the role. Or they weren't as academic as a sibling who had a straightforward career path. The result is a feeling of non-achievement or not being as good as others. There was never that moment of feeling we had achieved what we set out to do. Dare I say it, women (and we know that 97 per cent of assistants are women) are generally not comfortable blowing their own trumpet, because they think it sounds like bragging or showing off. We need to get over that and start understanding that this is now a profession and not just a job.

This book will inspire, motivate, challenge and excite you by exploring the opportunities that exist in this role when you understand your power and contribution.

Whether you are new to the role and want to understand what you should be aspiring to or a seasoned professional looking to reinvigorate and press reset, you are in the right place.

Conversely, what are the things that you're terrible at? What are the things that if they put them on your desk, you think, 'Oh, please don't give me that to do. It's not something I feel confident in tackling'? These are exactly the things we need to upskill in.

But finally, and most importantly, my fourth question is, when was the last time you felt highly motivated? I recently saw the graphic in Figure 0.1 and it shocked me. Sometimes seeing things graphically brings them to life.

FIGURE 0.1   Your work–life journey

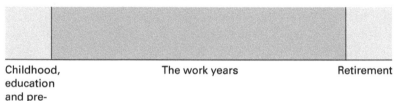

Childhood, education and pre-work life   The work years   Retirement

This graph shows three periods in your life. The first is a tiny segment right at the very beginning. It represents you from birth to age 16 (or 18 or 21, depending on when you finished your education). During this period, your parents constantly remind you that you can have a fantastic career if you work hard. At the other end of the graphic, there's another tiny segment of your life: retirement. Some of you spend your entire working life working towards retirement, and some of you won't even get there.

And in the middle is this huge piece, which is your work life. So, what is the point? What is the point if this segment does not make your heart sing?

If your reaction to my fourth question was, 'Not at the moment, that's for sure', I'm hoping that by the time you finish this book, I will have shown you a path that will make you fall in love with your job all over again, with your heart singing and excited to become reinvested in this career that you've chosen.

And make no mistake, it is a career now. It's not just a job. For the longest time, it was about turning up and doing tea and typing. But that isn't what it is anymore. The assistant role has moved on, and now, more often than not, you are strategic business partners to your managers, supporting them at the highest level.

CHAPTER ONE

A changing world and your place in it

So, where are we going to start?

Positioning where the profession is and why we find ourselves here seems like as good a place as any. Understanding the WHY before we get into the HOW is always helpful.

As human beings, we don't like change much. It scares us because we feel out of control. And yet, if I were to tell you that nothing in your life was ever going to change again, you would be horrified. It isn't the change itself that is the problem. It's the uncertainty and the speed with which it often happens.

This is a profession that is in an acute state of change. It's a bit like somebody has taken a pack of playing cards and thrown them up in the air. They have yet to land, and nobody is quite sure what it will look like when they do. But the great news is that we are creating what the future will look like for our profession, and each of us has our part to play. We need to get comfortable with being uncomfortable, not least because all sorts of things are at play here. It isn't just the profession changing; the world of work is also in a state of flux.

There have been assistants recorded back as far as Roman times. Cicero, Napoleon and George Washington, for example, all had secretaries. These people aren't to be confused with the personal secretaries that those leaders also had. Rather, they were close advisers who handled the most delicate strategic matters and became trusted confidants; the word 'secretary' means 'keeper of secrets'.

This was originally a male career. But then, during the Second World War, the men were called up to fight and the women stepped in. And they were so good at it that it is now a profession that is over 97 per cent female and employs over half a billion people globally. You make up a fifth of the world's working population.

Let's return to the 1940s when the role was very much 'tea and typing' and secretaries were part of a pool. You were expected to turn up and do as you were told. The role was entirely reactive. And, of course, over the years, the role changed as assistants took on more responsibility. Karen Nussbaum's 9 to 5 movement in the 1950s and the resulting collaboration on the film of the same name starring Jane Fonda helped change perceptions of female office workers for the better.

But in 2008, there was a seismic shift. The reason? Recession. Lehman's, one of the biggest investment banks in the world, went bang, and overnight, businesses let go of many of their middle management. And then they came to you and asked ever so nicely if you would take on some of the things the middle management did. There is nothing more permanent than temporary, so 87 per cent of assistants are still organizing events, 53 per cent are handling HR and many of you are doing finance, social media and marketing.

As far back as 2014, the American Society of Administrative Professionals surveyed its 70,000 members and proved that the assistant is the new middle management. For those of you that tell me you don't think you are an assistant anymore because you are juggling so many other things, this is, for many, the new role.

It's worth remembering when we talk about the impact of Covid-19 later in the chapter that during the recession, most assistants were asked to take on all sorts of things that they had no experience in, without training and with no pay rise. We were in survival mode and knuckled down. After all, we are the problem solvers, not the problem creators, and many were pleased to have the additional responsibility.

In many ways, for assistants, this recession was a good thing. It meant you were 'seen' for the first time. Many were able to partner at a far higher level or work in areas of the business not open to them before. Administrative directors took their places on boards – and with administration making up a fifth of the world's working population, this was absolutely what should have happened.

Before I move on to the second major change, I want to talk about Belbin. If you are unfamiliar, Belbin is a psychometric testing system developed by Meredith Belbin in the 1950s. The test shows how teams fit together, and Belbin says that there are nine different types of people in the ideal team. Some businesses take it so seriously that when someone leaves, they will only hire for that one strand.

I love Belbin because it's the simplest way to show why a business needs both an assistant and a manager.

It's important to remember that it's the business that employs you, not your manager. And have you ever asked yourself why your business employs you? It's to ensure that every minute of the manager's time and, therefore their salary, is best spent. You are a tool to increase efficiency. More of that later.

When we test managers and assistants using Belbin, we tend to fall into different but distinct categories. Managers fall into Shaper, Plant and Resource Investigator.

Shapers are parental in style; they don't care much if they upset people and are autocratic. It's their way or the highway.

Plants are cranial; they come up with new products or systems. Think of the genius, techy people you know. The problem is that they are often not the greatest communicators. Many of them should be kept in a high tower, coming up with ideas, but should not be allowed near people.

And then there are the Resource Investigators. These managers are charismatic; people will follow them to the ends of the earth. They are probably from a sales or marketing background. They thrive on driving the business forward and taking the rest of the staff with them on that journey of success. The problem is that they couldn't complete or finish anything if their lives depended on it. They are hopeless at the detail. If you have an RI manager, you are probably chasing them down the corridor, urging them to come back because they were due in a meeting 10 minutes ago, reminding them that their board report is now two days overdue.

The assistants typically fall into three just as important but very different categories that fill the managers' skills gaps.

The first is the Team worker. They thrive on ensuring everything is running smoothly and want everyone to be happy. Communication is key to their success. If they are working with a Shaper, they will usually be found reassuring other staff members not to take what the Shaper said personally. If they are working with a Plant, their role will be more of a 'translator' ensuring the Plant has what they need from everyone else.

Then there is the Completer Finisher. As you might expect, these are the 'detail' people. They dot the I's and cross the T's. In fact, they love detail so much that they often don't want to delegate because they think they are the only ones who can do it properly.

And thirdly, there is the Implementer, and this is where the assistant scores highly and comes into their own. The implementer does precisely what the name suggests. They take ideas and turn them into reality by putting the process and procedure in place to make them happen. Nobody else in the business thinks in quite this way. It is the assistant's major strength. As a CEO, can I do process and procedure? Of course I can, but quite frankly, I would rather stick pins in my eyes. It's just not how my mind works naturally; it takes a lot of concentration. It's why I have always had an assistant. It's also why my assistant will often go pale when I say I have had a fantastic idea. They know it will be them that will need to make it work.

So, can you see then that there are two worlds at play here – and two totally different skill sets? Neither is less important than the other, and the business needs both. Because when you work together, it's like the business has employed one complete and ideal employee. You are two sides of the coin. And when it's right, it's like one of you breathes in, and the other breathes out. It's magic.

The second major change is the fourth industrial revolution: automation, artificial intelligence and digitalization. It's not something that is coming. It's something we're right in the middle of. Even before Covid-19, we were telling you that you needed to:

a step up and make sure your digital skills are where they need to be
b make sure you have a better understanding of your business
c become more proactive

This has become even more critical post-Covid.

The World Economic Forum tells us that 50 per cent of businesses are accelerating automation, 83 per cent are scaling for remote work and 84 per cent are accelerating digitalization.

Post-pandemic, many of the most senior assistants that I know have told me that they had fallen behind with their digital skills because , at their level, technology had seemed increasingly unimportant in their roles, but they have had to get back up to speed – FAST.

Many of you will have seen the headlines in various press about how the role is set to disappear, and there is a grain of truth in that. To see why, we need to visit the new Global Skills Matrix from the World Administrators Alliance.

For those unfamiliar with the World Administrators Alliance, it's an umbrella organization for Administrators Associations worldwide. It organizes the World Administrators Summit, now held every two years, to discuss the most important issues to administrative professionals worldwide. It produces wonderful work guiding, developing, influencing and elevating the profession, including papers on The Identity and Image of Administrative Professionals, Diversity and Inclusion, The Career Behind the Job, Workplace Bullying and Mental Health. I was lucky enough to Chair the World Administrators Summit in 2015 in Papua New Guinea, have facilitated at many Summits since then and have been at the forefront of driving the concept of the Global Skills Matrix.

The Matrix took six years to complete, and was based on one of the most extensive pieces of research ever done into the profession, encompassing the views of assistants from 61 countries.

The results were shocking.

They showed that there were over 160 job titles, and that was just in the English language. This causes enormous confusion when it comes to how an assistant is employed, promoted and trained. In the UK, for instance, you might have a PA looking after reception or a PA looking after the CEO. An EA tends to be higher than a PA. In the United States, however, a PA tends to look after an individual of high net worth or a celebrity, with the term tending to be Administrative Assistant. And in Europe, the most common title is Management Assistant.

The research also showed that 58 per cent of assistants felt underutilized. To be clear, there is plenty of work to do. It's just that the level of support that they are being asked to give is often at a far lower level than what they are capable of. In fact, 73 per cent felt their organization didn't understand the role or the potential impact of using them properly. Sixty per cent felt there was little or no opportunity for career progression within their company. For many, the only way to get recognition was when their manager was promoted, and they went with them.

Clearly, something had to change. For the first time, we now have a global framework for career progression for the administrative profession. The matrix was signed off by the heads of associations from 29 countries, and the HR departments of some of the biggest companies in the world are restructuring their administrative functions because of it. They finally have a way to measure performance, implement succession planning, and set goals and KPIs for assistants. Traditionally, assistants have sat across the business and have been siloed and often overlooked when it comes to measuring return on investment. However, since the pandemic, as understanding the value of each employee becomes vital, HR departments are delighted to have this tool handed to them on a plate.

As you can see in Figure 1.1, the concept is straightforward. We have built five levels of assistant, with 1 being entry level and 5 being Chief of Staff. And then we have listed the skills and behaviours needed at each level to show how an assistant can progress through their career. There is a separate matrix for the tasks an assistant can be expected to do at each level. We have kept it simple on purpose. We want it to be instantly clear how it works.

Having no job titles means companies can map their assistants to the matrix and everyone can see where they sit. Every business can use it as a framework and guide to create a version that fits their business.

And what about assistants that want to stay at level 3, for example? Well, that is fine, of course, but this framework allows them to clearly see what excellence looks like at each level so they can strive to be the best level 3 possible.

FIGURE 1.1 Global Skills Matrix levels

1 Entry Level	2 Transactional	3 Transactional + Strategic	4 Strategic	5 Chief of staff
Reactive first role or returner	*Reactive*	*Reactive > Proactive*	*Fully Proactive*	*Leader*
• Communication skills – written, on the phone, and face to face • Technology – knowledge of office software e.g. Microsoft Office or Google equivalent • Basic social media • Organizational and planning skills • Attention to detail and accuracy • Information collection and management • Customer service orientation • Adaptability and flexibility • Teamwork • Discretion, confidentiality and integrity • Emotional intelligence • Problem solving • Self-motivated	• Knowledge of administrative procedures and processes • Strong communication skills • Knowledge of principles and practices of basic office management • Time management, prioritizing • Decision making • Ethical awareness • Cultural awareness	• Diplomacy and negotiation • Higher level communication skills • Foresight, anticipation, and initiative • People management • Digital fluency across a wide range of platforms • Design skills • Data analysis • Project/event management • Mentor/Coach • Understanding of the organization's and executive(s)'s objectives, goals, and KPIs • Resilience and stress tolerance • Delegation • Office co-ordination/ management e.g. budgeting, parking, vehicles and maintenance	• Usually board level/C-suite • Strategic planning • Critical thinking • Complex problem solving • Complex analysis and evaluation • Leadership • Leading projects • Ability to work autonomously • Understanding of all key business areas i.e.: risk management, business finance, marketing, HR, customer mangement, governance • Sector specific specialism or technical knowledge • Proactively supporting and driving the organization's and the executive(s)'s objectives, goals, and KPIs	• Broad understanding of all areas of the business • Internal facing role maximizing the efficiency and operations of the organization and CEO • Works with the CEO representing as required • Advanced research, analysis and briefing • Strategic thinking, understanding, and knowledge • Leadership and management expertise with organizational and strategic dexterity • Sensitivity of cultural diversity and inclusion • High level communication and interpersonal skills (esp. listening, tact, diplomacy, negotiation, problem solving, emotional intelligence, judgement, decision making) across all levels of the organization • High performing team building and relationship skills • Large/complex project management skills

SOURCE Global Skills Matrix (2021) reproduced with kind permission of World Administrators Alliance

You can read more extensively about this free resource and download all the supporting documents at www.globalskillsmatrix.com.

A word about job titles.

The brave amongst you are taking up the challenge and making the case for a career path for assistants within your organizations.

The flip side of this is that I'm seeing other assistants resisting a change to their job titles within their new structures. They want to continue to be an 'Executive Assistant' because it is a status symbol.

The truth is, as I said earlier in the chapter, there are over 160 titles for this job family. It's why the levels in the Global Skills Matrix were labelled 1–5, so that everyone could see themselves in it, and map their job title to it – whether that was their old one or a new variation.

The important thing is this. When there is no career framework, a job title is the only way to show seniority.

As career paths continue to evolve in your companies, your importance should not be tied to your former job title but should be measured through performance review and by your skills, competencies and behaviours.

If we are wanting to move away from our role being seen as a job rather than a career, and if we want to be seen as talent rather than a resource, we need to find better titles to explain what we do.

We are no longer assisting. We are doing.

Language has the power to change perceptions. Let's make sure we're using it to our advantage – and to the advantage of our businesses – by ensuring we are looking forwards to the new role, rather than getting hung up on old titles.

So back to the fourth industrial revolution and why there is a grain of truth in those articles that say assistants will disappear.

If you are a level 2, which is a reactive, task-based assistant, relying on people to tell you what to do, your role will eventually go. If you can do something the same way twice, you can automate it. And as we have already seen, businesses are increasingly automating processes. It's why becoming more strategic becomes so essential. Stepping into understanding your business, supporting at a higher level, and using automation to free you from the boring bits allows us to reinvent the role to fit the business needs.

Interestingly, the US Bureau of Labor Statistics only lists one level for assistants, which is level 2. Journalists have seized upon this to show that the role will disappear. Indeed, even the World Economic Forum lists the role as number 2 in the top 10 jobs that are disappearing. And yet, Glassdoor lists the EA as one of its top 10 roles of the future.

On the plus side, the WEF lists the skills that will be needed for the future of work as:

- problem solving
- self-management
- working with people
- tech use and development

The business press is talking about how the skills of the future will be human skills like resilience, attention to detail, emotional intelligence, service orientation, persuasion and negotiation. It sounds like an assistant to me! I don't think you're going anywhere, but understanding what businesses need and where your value sits is imperative.

And talking of understanding, someone needs to understand the processes before they can be automated, and someone needs to know how to implement the new technology. I would be becoming the IT department's best friend. Don't wait. Be proactive.

A recent student in her 60s shared that she was almost at retirement age but, with four years to go, didn't want to be put out to pasture just yet. She asked for advice. I suggested she talk to IT and study the latest advancements in Microsoft Teams and

Google Workspace, as well as keeping an eye on what apps are becoming available to enhance the assistant role. She has been keeping her internal network of assistants updated ever since and reports that their perception of her has changed completely.

The robots ARE coming but embrace that opportunity because it can only be good for your role. Embrace it because automation will free you up to step away from the repetitive, task-based work and into the more highly valued strategic work. And becoming an authority on what technology is coming down the track positions you to become a trusted advisor.

So, what is the third change? Of course, it was the pandemic. Covid-19 turned everything on its head. There is no new normal – yet. We are in the middle of creating it, and that brings uncertainty.

But one thing is sure. This is the best opportunity that you will ever have to recreate the role to be what you have always wanted it to be. Why? Because everything in the world of work just changed, so what's one more change?

You are the chaos tamers. We have already established that your strengths lie in detail, process and procedure. Right now, those skills have never been more critical. Nobody else in the business thinks quite that way. And your managers need to be freed up to do the work that the business is paying them to do, not the administrative detail around it.

At the start of the pandemic, you were falling into two groups. Half of you were coming and telling me that the middle management had been laid off, and you were expected to pick up a lot of their work, much of which you had never done before – sounding horribly familiar? It's precisely what happened in the 2008 recession. Hang onto your hats because, as we have already seen, this created increased recognition and opportunities for the assistant and changed the perception of the profession.

The other half of you were stressed and concerned. Many were working from home and felt invisible. The communication piece became non-existent, and you were left floundering in the dark, with many of you telling me that you were worried that your manager wasn't giving you anything to do. When you came out the other end of the pandemic, would they let you go?

I told those people, with love, to get a grip. Most of those managers were trying to recreate the world of work for their employees, to keep everyone safe and, in some cases, to save their companies. They didn't have time to think about what it was that you should be doing. So, when you went to them and asked, 'What should I do?', I suspect they thought, 'I don't care! Whatever it is that we pay you to do.' The clarity of why a manager needs a proactive assistant has never been more evident. And it has never been more important for a manager to tackle the work that they are actually being paid to do. In terms of the administrative work that they misguidedly clung onto, we shifted from whether they 'could' do that work to whether they 'should' be doing that work.

I would start thinking about 'the work' as a metaphorical pile of papers. The assistant should go through it and work out which bits they should handle and only give the critical work that they were unable to tackle to the manager.

I hope that by now you are starting to see why the assistant is a strategic business partner and to understand your value to your business. But we need to start to understand your value on a far deeper level.

Assistants often tell me that they don't get the same opportunities within their businesses as other members of staff because they don't contribute to the bottom line as the others do! What total and utter TOSH!

Let's do the math, shall we?

Firstly, how much does your manager earn?

Shall we agree that it's a lot!

And how much time do you save them as a percentage each week by doing things that they would otherwise have to do for themselves?

Shall we also agree on a lot?

After all, that's what you are employed to do, right? To give them back time so that the business maximizes the return on their salary.

So if you multiply one by the other, that is what you contribute to the bottom line.

And that is before they do work that will generate revenue in the time you have saved them. That is also what you add to the bottom line.

And that is before you do your actual job, which often involves researching the most cost-effective ways of doing things and negotiating.

So please don't tell me you don't contribute to the bottom line. You do! You bring enormous value to your businesses every day!

The other thing that a lot of you tell me is that you want to be seen as part of the core business. But if you're honest with yourself, do you see yourself that way and are you behaving like it?

Do you really understand the business, or do you just know a lot about it? There is a difference. Do you know what your executive's goals and KPIs are this year and how you can support them to get there?

Do you know what success looks like for them and what they are trying to achieve?

Have you made it your business to learn the language of business so you can make a confident contribution to the conversation?

Do you position yourself as part of the team, or do you see yourself as sitting outside it as 'support'?

Most assistants can explain at a surface level what is going on in their department, and give headlines about what their organization's goals are. But when challenged on what that means, or where their manager fits into the bigger picture, or what the numbers are around that, or what their individual contribution therefore needs to be, they suddenly realize how much learning they still have to do. We will explore this in a lot more detail in Chapter 7, when we look at business strategy and how to strategically manage your manager.

What matters most is how you see yourself! And that can mean a mind shift.

Have you ever asked yourself why businesses employ assistants? When I ask assistants and managers that question, the answers are usually along the lines of 'to support' or 'to do the stuff they don't want to do'.

This is categorically not the case.

One of the most important things for both you and your manager to understand about your role is that you are employed by your business – not by your manager. And you are employed by the business to ensure that every minute of the manager's time, every dollar of their salary, is best spent to maximize the return on investment.

You are the expert at being the assistant – they are not.

International speaker Bonnie Low-Kramen often quotes a statistic in her training from the entrepreneur Jack Zenger, which says that the average age someone gets management training is 46. That's a lot of management walking around with no clue what they are doing, and most are clear that they have never been trained on how to use an assistant. Personally, I think they could do with a module in business school, but that is a subject for another day.

So, if we now have clarity on what you are there to do, and we also understand that most executives have no idea how to best use you, I would challenge you that as it's the business that employs you, not the manager, YOU have a duty to train THEM on how to utilize you properly.

My first assistant was Elizabeth, or Bob as she liked to be called. I was 29 when they gave her to me, and I had just been made a publisher for the first time. I was thrilled. I went home and excitedly told my husband, 'They gave me an assistant'. I had no clue how to use her AT ALL. It was a status symbol. Luckily Bob was clear on what she was there to do and trained me how to use her. Most managers are not so lucky. I maintain that if the world's businesses used their assistants correctly, you could change the economy, eliminate burnout and improve work-life balance.

An author asked me recently for my favourite time management tip for a book she was writing and was astonished when I said, 'Get an exceptional executive assistant'.

You need to stop thinking about yourself as a gatekeeper of people and start thinking about yourself as a gatekeeper of time.

Laura Belgrado, one of Europe's top EA trainers and a former C-suite EA, told me that one day she was rummaging on her manager's desk, looking for something, when she came across his wage slip. In that moment, she realized two things. Firstly, she had to stop feeling sorry for him – he was more than compensated for the role that he chose to do. And secondly, she was managing him all wrong. She mentally worked out how much he was worth an hour and, from then on, made it her mission to shave as much time off every hour as she could – to give his time back to the company and free him up to do other things.

The serial entrepreneur Jeff Hoffman tells a great story that illustrates this point perfectly.

One night he went to dinner with an eminent heart surgeon friend of his by the name of Carl. When he arrived, Carl was sorting out his calendar for the next week. Jeff asked him what he was doing. Carl replied that he was organizing his calendar. Jeff was flabbergasted and responded, 'But aren't you worth $500 an hour?'

Jeff says that if you don't have an assistant, then you are an assistant. Just think about that for a moment. So, to all intents and purposes, Carl was paying his assistant $500 an hour to do his calendar.

How many things is your executive doing for themselves that the business is currently paying them their salary to do, that you should be doing for them instead?

Here is a great example of that.

Harvard Business Review tells us that the average CEO spends 24 per cent of their time on email (Porter and Nohria, 2018). That's 24 per cent of their salary that they are spending on email management. Most assistants want to manage their manager's email. It means they have a better understanding of what is going on in the business. All three of my assistants said they learned most from reading my sent emails. But the conversation often goes like this:

ASSISTANT: 'I know in the past you have been reluctant to let me manage your emails, but I am your assistant. I should be managing your email.'

MANAGER: 'No, thank you. I am perfectly capable of managing my own email. And anyway, there is confidential stuff in there that you really shouldn't see.'

What is really going on here?

The manager doesn't want to give up control. They want to write their own emails in their own tone. Maybe they don't trust you yet? Or perhaps they think it will take longer to explain to you how to answer than to do it themselves. They could be concerned you will delete things they need.

By the way, the confidential part is a red herring. You can always set up another email address for the confidential stuff.

We have a triage system that will take the amount of time they spend on email down to 12 per cent, freeing up 12 per cent of their time to do other things (and giving the company back 12 per cent of their salary). They will still be in total control and nothing will ever be deleted. I shall talk about that later in the book.

Are you starting to become clearer about your role and how you can add value and take on greater responsibility to become the trusted administrative business partner your manager needs?

The truth is that if you don't like change, you are going to like irrelevance even less. I see many assistants that prefer to keep their heads beneath the parapet. They hope it will all go away and that they can remain reactive, task-based and subservient. They never question anything. They report to their manager and they do as they are told.

But the future of the profession belongs to those who are proactive. They ask questions; the best assistants are endlessly curious. They really understand their businesses and how to communicate and collaborate effectively. They see themselves as managers, and a core part of their role is leading up – driving the agenda for their executives. They manage projects and explore where they can add more value so that they can make a more confident contribution to their businesses.

And that's important, especially post-pandemic, because increasingly businesses are being asked to measure the value of every member of staff. And for the very first time, businesses are approaching me asking how they prove the return on investment on their administrative function.

Businesses want to set goals and KPIs so that everyone understands what excellence looks like. They want to be able to measure the value that each assistant brings to the table. And of course, we are telling them how to do just that.

Businesses are also talking about how to structure better the way that they hire, promote and manage their assistants. And how they ensure the managers understand how to use their talents properly and how to make sure the right managers work with the right assistants. Hallelujah! It feels like the dam is starting to break.

We're in the middle of a perfect storm. The 2008 recession, the fourth industrial revolution and the pandemic have combined to create a window of opportunity for us to recreate the administrative role so that business understands the value that an assistant can bring to the table. But it needs to be you that makes that change. It's no good waiting for someone else to take the lead. Nobody else can do it for you.

You shall, you will and you must play your part. Otherwise, the moment will pass you by, and everyone else will have created a new world of work that leaves you behind.

Reference

Porter, M and Nohria, N (2018) How CEOs manage time, *Harvard Business Review*, July–August

Resource

Global Skills Matrix (2021) https://globalskillsmatrix.com/ (archived at https://perma.cc/M7JE-MNRW)

CHAPTER TWO

The network is all powerful

If you want to start changing perceptions about your role, one of the best ways to begin is to join or set up an internal assistant network.

The assistant role is a strange one.

Unlike other job groupings within the business, such as finance, sales or marketing, the executive support function doesn't usually have its own department. Instead, you work horizontally across your businesses and therefore are often siloed. This leads to non-collective thinking and often there is no cohesive plan or leadership for assistants.

Or, as Brian Tracy, author of *Eat the Frog*, so eloquently puts it, 'No one lives long enough to learn everything they need to learn starting from scratch. To be successful, we absolutely, positively have to find people who have already paid the price to learn the things that we need to learn to achieve our goals' (Tracy, 2012).

It's telling that when we run Executive Support LIVE events, one of the most common pieces of feedback we get is, 'Thank goodness it's not just me. I thought I was the only one dealing with that problem and that I must be doing something wrong.'

Can you imagine finance or marketing with no leadership? It's unthinkable. So why is it OK for a business's administrative professionals? Time and again, I see businesses with no career path, no performance review, no succession planning and no value measurement for assistants. In fact, in many companies, particularly in the United States, the only way to get promoted is to move up the ladder when your executive does.

In her excellent article 'The need for inclusion', Simone White explains how time and again in our profession, we see examples of a lack of inclusion, some so ingrained they are viewed as 'normal' and 'acceptable'. Simone explores how this lack of visibility results in exclusion for administrative professionals, even where structures do exist to increase inclusion, and argues that it is only by being seen, heard and valued as a group that our profession will remain viable.

And yet, Maslow's Hierarchy of Needs (Figure 2.1) tells us that after our needs for the basics like air, water and food, and once our safety and belonging needs are met, the two other things we need as human beings to keep us happy are self-esteem and self-actualization. In other words, the need to be respected, recognized, to have status and to strive to become the best that we can be.

Quite apart from that, we need to be constantly evolving in order to survive because everything is changing so fast, not just within our roles but within the world of work. The World Economic Forum's Future of Jobs report (2022) says that 50 per cent of the working population will need retraining before 2025.

Assistants all over the world are taking matters into their own hands and setting up internal assistant networks with varying degrees of success.

Structuring your network properly is key to its success. It takes planning, clarity on what you want it to be, and buy-in and input from your peers and the management. Where I see

FIGURE 2.1   Maslow's Hierarchy of Needs (1943)

Self-Actualization
(need for development,
creativity)

Ego
(need for self-esteem, power,
recognition, prestige)

Social
(need for being loved, belonging, inclusion)

Security
(need for safely, shelter, stability)

Physical
(need for air, water, food, rest, health)

internal networks fail is where the assistants that set it up don't understand what the network is for.

A network is not an excuse for a monthly social event or a place to moan about frustrations. Nor is it somewhere for HR or IT to come and talk about the latest thing that they would like you to be doing.

Rather, it is an opportunity to ensure the administrative functions are fully utilized and as efficient as they can be. Businesses need exceptional administrative support at all levels and in lieu of the businesses themselves putting structure in place, the internal assistant network is a start. It creates a cohesive unit amongst the executive support function. You are able to share best practices, assume an identity, run training and work more efficiently, saving time and money for your company.

The best place to start is by looking at what the business needs. As with all things, when you show management what is in it for the business or for them personally, they are far more likely to buy into it. How will it save time and money? Where is the evidence of increased efficiencies? How will it benefit them?

Show them how you intend to create a world-class administrative function that will underpin what the stakeholders are trying to achieve; that will save cost and time by making managers and executives more productive and efficient.

As Cathy Harris, the world authority on internal assistant networks, explains in her book *The Executive Support Guide to Creating an Internal Assistant Network*:

> An Internal Assistant Network will add a tremendous amount of value to all aspects of the assistant's role. Money is saved on training as this is now a shared value support network facilitated by the experts amongst you. We become more productive because we are saving time by having quick and effective access to resources, and one of our most important initiatives is that of creating and maintaining standards right across the board, ensuring our organization's reputation is aligned to a good work ethic, a great brand, and teamwork. Everyone is on the same page and working together collectively as a team. An Assistant Network offers the opportunity for the assistant to become a superstar in their role because they are constantly informed by it and actively participate in its success.

When assistants start from this perspective, they have no problem when they request a budget or time out of the office for training because the managers understand what's in it for them.

I work with many companies to help them to set up their internal networks and the most successful ones have:

- set up a team of dedicated and passionate assistants to lead it
- taken time to write a proposal that included clear objectives
- demonstrated the return on investment to the business
- planned a calendar of networking and training events for the year featuring external as well as internal speakers

- ensured that before they started, they had buy-in from the powers that be
- managed the expectations of both the management and the other assistants

One of the best networks I have come across is The Empowered Assistant Network at Janssen (a Johnson & Johnson company), based in Belgium. The first time I heard about it, I had a moment of total clarity. It was presented at a conference I attended, and I remember thinking, 'This is the missing piece. This is how networks should operate.'

Danielle De Wulf, the presenter, was one of 230 management assistants who supported 5,000 colleagues in different sites in Belgium and the Netherlands. What impressed me most was that right from the beginning they created their network with the aim of futureproofing their assistants. They consistently look at the skillsets needed to ensure their assistant network is a world-class administrative function.

Danielle told me:

Our story started in 2010. There was a lot of dissatisfaction in the administrative team. Depending on who the manager was, we had too much or not enough work to do. Some experienced more flexibility than others to attend training and international meetings and the ability to work from home occasionally was entirely at the discretion of the individual manager.

Vacation was not enjoyable because we were worried about the amount of workload when returning to our desks. Sometimes we missed career opportunities because we were informed too late or were unaware of the vacancy.

We decided to join forces and created a network community with approximately 30 admins.

We started by sharing info, tips and best practices, and, later, also workload. The other 200 admins gradually realized they were missing out on updates, opportunities and vacancies, so we expanded. Since 2015, all of our admins in Belgium and the Netherlands are part of one of our 15 teams.

Our smallest team is eight admins and the largest one 35 colleagues. Sometimes a team comprises all admins in one location or from the same department, sometimes it is cross-departmental, whatever works best.

For each team, we appointed team leads: volunteers wanting to explore their leadership skills in a safe environment. These 'captains' meet monthly to discuss what is new and solve workload issues.

Extra flex pools support our teamwork. We have an internal flex team of seven admins with a permanent contract, but their mission is to solve temporary needs. We compare them to the flying doctors from the Australian TV show because they go and help where there is an issue, like a peak in workload or because a colleague is on pregnancy or sick leave.

These flying assistants are very experienced and extremely flexible; they love change and adapt quickly. Since they help in many different departments, they pick up best practices and have the mandate to propose efficiency enhancements across the whole team.

In 2017 we started another experiment, with a hub of admins doing travel and expense notes for different departments. By clustering routine jobs that can be outsourced, admins can focus on the tasks where they can really make a difference. This lets us build an empowered network to become a future-proof, flexible, efficient and engaged self-steering community.

Our different talents and interests are the strength of our network. We create opportunities to meet, share info and learn from each other.

We also organize 'lunch & learn' sessions with inspirational speakers, sometimes external speakers but also any admin wishing to share knowledge or passion. So, we all learn and grow.

To share our learnings, we created ECAN (Empowered Community Admin Network), which is our own communication platform, where we post news, tips, updates, agendas for admin events and training, and growth opportunities. We communicate in a transparent way to all at the same time. The ECAN archive gives people a way to retrieve information easily.

By connecting internally, we help each other, resulting in quick wins and time savings. For example, we discovered it is more efficient to let one or two colleagues give a resume of procedural changes to their colleagues rather than having each admin work their way through the entire manual. If several managers attend the same congress, it's more efficient to centralize travel bookings and registrations rather than have admins arrange the trip for their manager only.

We connect externally with schools that provide education to office management students, the admins of the future; we organize company tours and offer them traineeships. We give the event management students the opportunity to work out a real-life event for us. Their teachers also join our training or speaker sessions, creating unique dynamics.

In return, the students' teachers keep us up to date on social media, presentation skills or other skills that were not part of our school training years ago.

We take stock of our strengths and talents. We check what competencies our job will require towards 2025. We put a training plan to close that gap and prepare all admins for the future.

These trainings range from technical skills to soft skills to project management and leadership skills. All our admins are encouraged to follow at least two trainings per year; they can choose one individually and the other one is mandatory with their team.

We developed a Train the Admin Programme: new admins are trained and brought up to speed by an experienced colleague who is a certified trainer. This on-the-job training by their expert colleagues represents huge time and energy savings for the hosting department. We changed our objective, from training only admins to training all functions, because management are increasingly expected to do admin work themselves, like booking travel.

Several development programmes are available in our company but addressed to managers, therefore we recreated them for admins. In our mentoring programme, the admin is coached by a director or someone at a higher level but the mentee is always in the driver's seat (e.g. use a mentor to learn how to give impactful presentations).

In our rotation project, two admins swap departments temporarily or explore new horizons via an international experience. Or they can sign up to participate in language lunches to practice French, Spanish, German, English and Italian.

What's in it for the admin?

- We are no longer working solo. We have an extensive network to help us.

- We save huge amounts of time because we can share best practices.

- There is transparency in opportunities and trainings.

- There are more growth and development possibilities and we are encouraged to make best use of our talents in our career path.

- This results in a better work-life balance and everyone has more fun and satisfaction in the job.

To foster this cooperation instinct, the right mindset is needed. We created an atmosphere of openness and trust, which avoids counterproductive job protection. It is safe to step out of our cocoon, it is rewarding to help each other, and it is more efficient to communicate and share best practices and to avoid duplication of work.

What does our admin network model mean to management?

- We offer business continuity and flexibility.

- We propose innovative workload and process solutions.

- The wheel is not being reinvented, which results in considerable cost and efficiency savings.

- We have the strongest network and communication platform across departments and sites.

How do we offer workload solutions with our flex pools and guaranteed business continuity?

The team lead or captain is the single point of contact for the group, which makes it easy for managers when they have any issues related to workload. We have a back-up system for expected and unexpected absences, so business continuity is guaranteed. We make smart use of idle time.

We dare to speak up, even about workload: if we have a dip because it is holiday season or our manager is on a business trip, we say so and help others out or take on a project. In return, we receive help when we have a peak in our workload. We strive for a fair workload and work pressure for every admin, based on interests, talents, capabilities and ambitions. It's therefore crucial that the team lead and supervisor know what their admins want in order to match their interests with the business needs.

How do we simplify, streamline or improve processes?

There are about 35 different administrative systems at Janssen. As system experts we quickly notice inefficiencies. Suggestions for improvement are embraced. We assemble a team with expert admins, business partners and all the right stakeholders. Together, they try to find a solution that saves time, energy and money for all, and this solution is communicated via ECAN, our dedicated admin website.

We have tackled over a dozen processes, solving problems with travel or expense receipts and streamlining procedures company-wide. In fact, one-third of our 180 admins are participating in one or more process groups on top of being part of a team. Indeed, lots of colleagues are thrilled to take ownership and more responsibility and to enlarge their circle of influence.

Eager to start your own internal network? Here are the ingredients

Our robust framework is highly customizable because it's modular and reproducible in all kinds of settings and companies. Just pick what would work in your company.

1 Find believers!
    ○ You need management and HR buy-in.
    ○ A dedicated person with an entrepreneurial spirit takes the lead of the admin team.
    Quick adaptors will understand the benefits, and more sceptical colleagues will follow as they realize that they will miss a lot if

they don't join. You will need time if you don't want to impose your model but let it grow bottom-up.

2 Ask for a budget
This money is to be spent on training and development and be sure to show what the return on investment will be. A guide to how to do this is shown later in the chapter.

3 Realize some quick wins:
- Make a distribution list of all admins in your company.
- List your system experts.
- Get together in groups and learn from each other. You'll be amazed how you pick up things your colleagues do differently.
- Organize informal lunches with brainstorming on how to solve inefficiencies.
- Make sure all members inform their team lead about their strengths, talents, interests and ambitions so they can match the company's needs with the talents onboard.
- Show metrics to earn trust from your management.
- These metrics can be about budget, time and/or energy savings and 'fewer frustrations'.

It's worth mentioning that if you don't have an internal network, either because you work on your own at your business or because it is not currently on the agenda, there are an enormous number of external networks and associations specifically for assistants right across the globe. And of course, even if you DO have an internal network, these groups are worth their weight in gold when it comes to making connections and futureproofing your career.

Executive Support Magazine lists every association that we have managed to track down so far on our website. Thousands of assistants across the world meet regularly via these associations and networks to socialize, educate themselves and keep up to date with the latest thinking. The list can be found at https://executivesupportmagazine.com/associations/.

As businesses re-evaluate and recreate the world of work, it's never been more important to focus on the money. It has become increasingly important to be able to prove the value that every employee delivers to a business in a quantifiable way. For the first time, in many cases, this includes the assistants.

For too long, businesses have seen assistants as sitting outside of what's going on in the main body of the business. They are seen as 'support' whereas, in reality, when assistants are trained to understand the potential of their role and become part of the business as true strategic business partners to their executives, that shift directly and positively drops to the bottom line.

But I would go one step further. Coming out of the pandemic – and bearing in mind that with most people working from home, none of the business functions sit together in departments anymore – isn't it time to look at creating 'administrative departments' instead of networks?

Because whilst networks go some way towards creating an administrative team, renaming that team a 'department' gives a totally different perception. Departments have a structure, a budget, clear business goals and objectives, proper training and performance metrics. It suggests specialization and skill. Unlike a network, it doesn't sit outside the business to be fitted in around 'real' work.

For the thousands of businesses talking to us every year about how to restructure their administrative functions to ensure they are fully utilizing their skills properly, a network has been an excellent first step. But setting up a department for the administrative function is the path to integration and inclusion within the core business. Not to mention that when done properly, it can yield enormous returns.

A recent company that I dealt with had over 500 assistants. None of them had been employed through HR, so there were over 60 job titles, and the job descriptions were woeful. Generic didn't even begin to cover it. The reliance on the well-worn phrase 'and anything else we might like to throw at you' meant that in reality, there was nothing to measure performance against. Add into the mix that each assistant was managed by their manager, who usually knew nothing about the profession, and it was a recipe for haemorrhaging the company's money.

The resulting administrative network creation and restructure, which was aligned with the Global Skills Matrix, meant that the company was able to achieve the following:

- Clarity on the ROI (return on investment) and value to the business of each admin.
- Uniformity and a level playing field in the way each administrative employee is treated.
- Pay based on performance not tenure – pay grades based on level achieved rather than time served or executive's personal preference.
- The ability for the company to test for level and skills gaps.
- Recruitment costs came down because everybody understood what the company needed to hire for.
- There was an alignment of skills with needs.
- Hours were saved for the managers because the assistants were properly trained.
- Performance review was streamlined.
- Succession planning was put in place.
- A clear career progression model was developed.
- It created a roadmap for what excellence looks like at every level.
- Clear goals and KPIs were established for each admin.
- A roadmap for training and development was implemented.
- There was finally clarity of the role for each employee – job descriptions were based on competencies.

The change in perception for the assistants within this company was, as you can imagine, game-changing. But it also had a huge impact on the bottom line.

Here's how you do the calculations to prove the cost benefits to your company.

You should find out from HR how much, on average, the middle management is paid. And how many of them there are.

You then need to calculate how much that works out to be per hour. We used a calculation that they were working 8 hours a day and 48 weeks a year.

Multiply the average amount per hour by the number of middle management.

In the case of the above company, it allowed us to show that if an assistant saved each of the middle management just one hour a day because of the restructuring and training implemented, this equated to a massive $88,640 saving per week.

This is before we look at higher-level managers and what they are paid.

This is before we look at what the management will spend their time doing in that time saved, which might generate revenue.

This is before we look at what the ACTUAL amount of time is that the fully trained assistants would save their executives every day.

This is before we look at savings in recruitment costs.

This is before we start paying salaries based on performance rather than tenure.

And this was before we found the superstar assistants currently hidden from view because there was no effective performance review system, and the people they were working for didn't understand how to utilize them best or what they are capable of.

When you put it in these terms, why wouldn't you make the change?

However, driving a change programme like this requires leadership and collaboration skills and that's where we're heading next.

References

Harris, C (2017) *The Executive Support Guide to Creating an Internal Assistant Network*, Marcham Publishing

Maslow, A (1943) A Theory of Human Motivation, *Psychological Review*, 50, pp 370–96

Tracy, B (2012) *Earn What you are Really Worth*, Vanguard Press

White, S (2022) The need for inclusion, *Executive Support Magazine*, 25 January

World Economic Forum (2022) The Future of Jobs Report 2022, https://www.weforum.org/reports (archived at https://perma.cc/VFH9-9RX3)

CHAPTER THREE

The assistant as an influential leader

M ost assistants don't see themselves either as influential or as leaders. But this couldn't be further from the truth, and to become an administrative business partner to your manager, you absolutely have to become both. But that means a change in mindset.

An assistant's job is to lead up, but there is a misconception that leading up is bad.

This is usually for one of three reasons. Firstly, you are concerned that if you try to lead up, the manager might take offence and think you are getting above yourself.

Or you might worry that they might think that you are trying to micromanage them because you don't trust them or their ability to do certain things properly.

Or it could be that it simply hasn't been how it is done in your company; maybe there has always been a culture of assistants being reactive and waiting to be told what to do. This is usually because nobody at your company has ever seen the benefits of a proactive assistant and it has never occurred to them to use you differently. But that is all about to change.

I have to tell you as a CEO myself, having an assistant that you trust, who leads up and allows you to get on with the things that you are good at, can't be undervalued. My EA, Fran, ticks all these boxes. My company is still really small, only 10 people. Can you imagine if Fran had to ask me for permission before she did anything? Or if she was waiting to be told what to do? I would not have a business. Fran runs everything whilst I am away and keeps me informed of what I need to know.

The trust is total – to such an extent that on one occasion when I had been travelling non-stop for two months and was extremely tired, I went to London Heathrow to catch yet another flight. The woman behind the counter at British Airways asked me where I was going – and do you know, I had no idea. I knew it was America, but I also knew that when I looked in my travel pack, every minute detail would be there, and I had no need to know it. Imagine for your manager what an incredible resource that is.

My strength is standing up in front of audiences of assistants and inspiring them. I want to do that for as many assistants as I possibly can, so having a team that does everything else is not just a preference but essential. Fran conducts the orchestra for me and makes sure everyone knows what they are meant to be doing and that it all happens at the right time. I was heading to Phoenix, by the way, in case you were interested.

I also want to touch on the term 'Servant Leadership'. On occasion, when I use the term, audiences get upset because they see the 'Servant' and not the 'Leadership' part. There is nothing derogatory about this term. I class myself as a servant leader. My role is to serve the administrative community to ensure that you are the very best that you can be. To provide support, mentorship, encouragement and tools. What you do for your managers is exactly the same. You are employed to make sure that they are the very best that THEY can be.

Before we go any further, let's talk about the difference between collaboration and teamwork. Much is currently being written about collaboration. It's a real buzzword, and it's important you understand it because, for assistants in particular, it changes everything.

Teamwork is the way we used to work, and collaboration is the working style of the future (see Figure 3.1). The best way for me to explain the difference is to use an analogy: putting on a theatrical play.

Let's look at teamwork first. When you work as a team to put on a play, you will have stage managers, costume designers, set designers, lighting and sound engineers, actors and, of course, the director. All of you have your own individual skill sets. And when you come together for the first day of rehearsal, the director will have a clear idea as to what you are trying to achieve. The key point here is that the director has control. You don't have to like the director in order to get the job done. There are clear roles and responsibilities and you all work together to deliver what the director needs.

Collaboration is totally different because it's not just about working together; it's about thinking together. On the first day of rehearsals for the play, everyone rocks up and sits down as a collaborative to work out how to put on the best play possible using all of their skill sets. The end product comes from the work of the group. There must be trust and respect, but there must also be clarity on what the end goal is. In the case of collaborative working, if the goal is not clear, the whole process descends into chaos.

It used to be that the assistant–manager relationship was unequal. In some cases, it could even have been compared to a master and servant relationship, but it isn't that way anymore. If you think back to what we said about Belbin, you both bring your unique and valuable skills to the table to make sure the business has what it needs to get the job done.

Why is this particularly important now? Everything that I am reading about the future of work suggests that 9 to 5 will eventually go. It was a concept invented by the Ford Motor

FIGURE 3.1   Teamwork vs collaboration example

Teamwork

- Working as individuals
- Clear roles
- Identified tasks
- Strong leader
- Don't need to like each other
- Control is key
- Leader drives team towards its goal

Collaboration

- Not only working together
- But also thinking together
- End product comes from the efforts of the group
- Equal partners
- Trust and respect
- What's the best result for the business – let go of ego
- Creative and flexible – give and take
- Must have a clear end goal

Company in 1926, but now that the majority of us are hybrid working, we will be shifting more towards goals being the new point of reference. As long as you achieve your goals within a timeframe, your business will be happy, and you will be able to work with much more flexibility.

It means taking ego out of it and doing what's best for the business as equal partners, each contributing your very different but complementary skill sets. It also means being creative and flexible in your approach and open to new ways of thinking and working. But most importantly, it requires that you understand what the goals are so that you can drive the agenda when it comes to the administrative processes and procedures required to achieve them. It's why I stress throughout the book that you need to be clear on what your manager's goals and KPIs are for the year. But also why you need to meet regularly to clarify what the daily and weekly goals are and how those have changed since the last meeting.

Let's go back to leadership. What kind of words come to mind when you think of a leader? What skills does an exceptional leader need?

I've been keeping track of what assistants tell me when we do this exercise in a classroom environment, and here are the top 15 words/phrases:

1   Integrity
2   Confident
3   Trusted
4   Authentic
5   Influential
6   Listener
7   Communication
8   Decisive
9   Emotional intelligence
10 Self-awareness
11 Perseverance

12 Takes responsibility
13 Empathy
14 Humble
15 Respect

Sounds like an assistant to me!

The way leadership is viewed has changed totally in the time I have been in the workplace. It is no longer about being out in front, leading the charge. It has become about influence, rather than authority. I love this quote from philosopher and writer, Lao Tzu: 'A leader is best when people barely know he exists; when his work is done, his aim fulfilled, they will say: we did it ourselves.'

Isn't that what you do every day? You lead up, and you do it so effectively that nobody notices the huge amount of time and effort that you put in to support your manager. In future chapters, particularly 6 and 7, we will look in more detail at how to do this most effectively.

But first, let's look at a few of the world's famous leaders and their assistants. What did the leaders teach their assistants and how did those assistants lead up?

The first is Zelda La Grange, Nelson Mandela's secretary, gatekeeper and constant companion for the best part of 20 years.

The first time a 20-year-old Zelda La Grange became aware of Nelson Mandela was when the announcement of Mandela's impending release was made by President FW de Klerk in February 1990.

So how did a young Afrikaner girl go from middle-class obscurity and a blindly ignorant apartheid past to become Mandela's constant companion and honorary granddaughter?

Zelda spent 19 years winning the affection, respect and trust of the black man who was once the most feared enemy of her family but became one of the greatest political figures of our time.

She began work as an anonymous typist in the presidential office in 1994, having originally applied for a typist job in the economics department. But before she knew it, she had been appropriated by Mandela's private secretary, Mary Mxadana, who was desperate for people who could type. Zelda became a typist on the President's personal staff.

It was just two weeks later that she bumped into him for the first time when she popped into his office to pick up a document:

> They say that to speak to the heart of a person you should speak in their language. The first time I met Madiba, he put out his hand to shake mine and spoke to me in Afrikaans. He asked me about myself and his kindness was overwhelming. I was so emotional that I cried uncontrollably.

He told her she was overreacting but La Grange says that she was scared of him, not knowing what to expect of him, whether he was going to dismiss her or possibly humiliate her:

> Instantly it was that feeling of guilt that all Afrikaners carry with them… He was 75 at the time, and you could see he was old and the thing that immediately crosses your mind is, 'I sent this man to jail'. My people sent this man to jail! I was part of this even though I couldn't vote. I was part of this, of taking from a person like him his whole life away. And then I started crying. And then he shook my hand, and he held my hand.
>
> After a few minutes I settled down, maybe smiled, and then he started asking me questions. Where had I grown up? What my parents did? We ended up talking for about five minutes. But it wasn't special treatment he was giving me. He would talk to all members of the staff, black and white, in the same way when he met them, asking them about their backgrounds, their families…

Her big break came in 1995 when he asked her to go to Japan with him. Mandela knew it was important at that time to show the world he was going to embrace all cultures, that he was going to have white people working with him.

La Grange believes that if someone believes in you, you need to take that forward:

> Madiba was the best coach and mentor. As a female Afrikaans-speaking person in the Office of the Presidency, I endured my fair share of criticism. One day Madiba said to me: 'If you're going to be a coward, you're not going to last in this office.' He always supported and believed in me, and I've learnt so much from him. The way in which he deals with people who stand in front of him has completely changed my life.

She went on to take on more and more duties for Mandela, regularly working 18-hour days, which left little time for any kind of life outside of the job:

> He started calling me to do more and more duties for him personally, to type letters, to be present at meetings, to take notes. Then in 1996 he insisted that I go with him on his state visit to France – still being the typist, but this time he did not take any of the other secretaries. I suddenly found myself having to perform the only secretary's duties abroad. And this time I really had to work and learn how things were done, what a state visit consists of, what we have to do.
>
> And after that I got more involved, with things around his private life, for example. And he would insist on me going here, there and everywhere with him – for example, when he went to visit a typical Afrikaner community, he wanted me to be there with him. In his eyes, I personified the typical Boer, and that was just fine with me. I was learning.
>
> My title was changed to assistant private secretary. As president he'd work very hard. He'd be up at one o'clock, two o'clock in the morning taking and making phone calls, sometimes right through the night and never catching up on lost sleep. I was always there, quick to respond. I could trace anyone on earth by telephone in record time. It helped that I was at an age where I had lots of energy and no commitments other than my work.

It was not a role that everyone could do – especially with all that hard work going unrecognized by Mandela's adoring public. The press, rather unflatteringly, regularly referred to her as 'The Rottweiler' because of her uncompromising protection of him. But La Grange says that's just the life of an assistant.

'It's not only about being an assistant; it's about being a backbone to someone', she says:

> You have to support someone, even if putting on the kettle will make his life better. It can't be limited to a job description. I was quite content with serving him because I could see how much my commitment meant to him, and he inspired loyalty. I got the credit from him that I needed, and that's more than enough. That's more than anyone can ask for.

At the end of his presidency, Zelda went with Mandela into retirement, becoming his private secretary. In all, she was at his side constantly for 19 years.

It has been well documented that in the run-up to his death in 2013, members of Mandela's family blocked Zelda from saying goodbye properly. She had been fully committed to him, always had his best interests at heart and had even sacrificed several friends and relatives who couldn't understand her unwavering loyalty to him. So having given up dreams of having a family, a husband or any life outside of serving Mandela for 19 years, was it worth it?

> At the age of 23 I wanted to marry and have three children. I wanted three boys actually. But life will take you where you're supposed to be. I had a choice – marriage and children or being part of history. I'm very grateful that I ended up having the opportunity to serve him. Regret is a useless emotion. It's a ship that has sailed – and I'm quite content.

These are sentiments she seemingly learned from Mandela himself, who she describes as 'the most unbelievable boss'.

When he died, she released a statement saying that: 'As sad as it makes me that I will never walk into a room again and see his generous, infectious smile or hear him say, 'Oh Zeldina, you are here', I have come to terms with the fact that Madiba's legacy is not dependent on his presence', adding: 'Thank you for believing in me, Khulu, making me a better person, a better South African.'

My second assistant is Ann Hiatt. Ann has worked as an executive assistant to three of the world's top tech giants: Jeff Bezos, Marissa Mayer and Eric Schmidt. She has just published her first book, *Bet on Yourself*.

Ann didn't start off working as an assistant. She originally wanted a career in academia. Her father and his brothers were farmers, but unusually, they all had at least a master's degree. From her early childhood, her family didn't talk about if they would go to university; it was when and what she was going to study.

Her plan was to be a professor. She set that goal for herself when she was really young. Her first job was working for a start-up before that term had even been coined. She worked for a five-person start-up in Redmond, Washington, and just wore all the hats learning what a start-up was. That was while she was still in high school, before she went to university. She did all sorts of bits and pieces which she didn't know were preparing her for that first big job.

At the tender age of just 20, she landed a job at Amazon, working for Jeff Bezos – a CEO who had been on the front cover of *Time*. Looking at his desk on day one, she saw he had reading material – a couple of magazines and a book – and decided to go and buy copies of all three of them. From that day on, she continued to purchase and read everything he did. What an amazing way of getting inside someone's head.

Ann says:

Jeff was a voracious reader, minimum of a book a day. How he did that, I don't know because we were working 18-hour days pretty regularly, but every morning he would come in with three completely read newspapers under his arm: the *Wall Street Journal*, the *New York Times*, and the *Seattle Times*. He would put them down on his desk and then I would take them, and I would devour them during my lunch break, read all of them cover to cover. And any book he was reading at the moment, I would then take. Literally everything, briefing documents, every email in his inbox. I would listen to every phone call and take notes on what I understood or what I wanted to dive into more.

When you are trying to support someone, you really need to become their brain double; you need to be able to mind read, and I knew that I was so far removed from being able to do that in the beginning that I just had to consume as much of the information that he had as was possible, so I had that foundational context. Then I could strive to become more proactive, to make recommendations and see around blind corners, but first I just had to build up a very firm foundation of the industry knowledge that I did not have when I started.

Ann learned very different things working for Marissa Mayer:

The first two things that come to mind are that Marissa really modelled and demanded that people do things before they felt ready. Before working for Marissa, I thought being ready to take on a new challenge meant being ready to do it perfectly. Marissa taught me that being ready for a new challenge is just being willing to raise your hand. She created a safe space where it was OK for you to just do your best and run really fast and learn. As long as you were learning – pivot, iterate, try it again, over and over again. She had no expectation that we should do it perfectly.

In fact, in my very first performance evaluation, her major critique of me (which at the time really hurt my feelings and is one of the greatest business lessons anyone has ever given me) was that I was playing it way too safe. I was hitting all my targets, I was accomplishing all my goals, and to her that was more of a failure than setting enormous goals that I was barely scratching the surface of. She allowed me to set goals for myself that terrified me. And I was allowed to learn. When you shoot for the stars and hit the moon, that's success. That is the kind of environment that she built.

The second biggest lesson that I took away, and I still think about today, is the way she built teams. She was so talented in identifying early rough stages of talent and investing in those people, polishing them, giving them huge challenges to accelerate their learnings. The people that she hired back in 2006, 2007, 2008 now run the major tech companies. Either they are major executives within Google, or they have gone on to run tech companies that you and I use every day. She was just a spectacular identifier of talent and invested heavily in that. She was our greatest champion.

Then Ann pivoted again and joined Eric Schmidt, Google CEO, as his EA. It was obviously different again to working with Jeff or Marissa. Ann explained what the main differences were:

Eric is an incredibly unique individual. There are many common denominators between those three, but Eric is more of an academic. He has a PhD. The other two have master's degrees, but Eric is a PhD graduate. He also went to Berkeley, the same as I did. He is just more thoughtful, contemplative and laid back.

'Professor mode' is his usual stance in a meeting, where he encourages and pulls out the unique voices in the room. He is very data-driven in his decision making. And then, when he speaks, you can see everyone in the room lean in. He waits until he has got all the data he needs, and he calls on the quietest voices in the room (which is a terrifying thing the first time you are in a room with Eric – you are not expecting that).

And then he is a statesman. That was a really important quality for the difficult job he was hired to do. I do not know of any other company that had co-founders that hired a professional CEO to come in and implement their vision. Eric never forgot that Google was not his company, and I point that out because that really shaped the way he performed his role as a CEO: it was Larry and Sergey's company – he was there to maximize their vision, to hone it and to break it down into manageable steps because of his background and expertise, but he made their vision come to light. And I think that is why this trifecta leadership worked so beautifully. They challenged each other, and they were very aggressive and honest with each other. But Eric always leaned back and made sure it was their vision that was being implemented, and I have never seen anyone else be able to do that in the way that he did.

Ann very famously created the role of Chief of Staff at Google for herself. It was not something that had previously existed. Now Chief of Staff is the term that so many companies are using for that level. Ann explained how she created that role and why:

It took years of kicking and kicking against the glass ceiling that was in front of me. Google is amazing. They were the industry leaders in developing the admin and support structure of the company, recognizing that's the skeleton of the company, that what holds everything up is this administrative support, so we were respected. I think at the time, every single one of us had minimum master's degree education. We were considered thought partners to our executives. We had to be brain-double-level worthy, so all of us were performing at extremely high levels, but I saw an opportunity to expand it beyond that.

I saw the Chief of Staff role from my friends in government. I was doing a lot of collaborative projects with people in policymaking, and Chief of Staff is something that exists within the politics world in the United States and comes from a military influence. But I saw the way in which they were anticipating, they were leaning into the strategy work, they were representing their policymakers in rooms when they were not there. I saw an opportunity to really 10x Eric's output by behaving in the same way. So, I went to HR, and I advocated for this role. I wrote the description, I did case studies, I modelled it. I took on that role before they officially gave me permission to do so. And I came back and gave them the data: the results we were getting because of this behaviour shift, what I was able to do, the 10x results that we had got. I asked, 'Why don't we create an additional layer on this ladder to recreate and recognize that?' I got 'Nos' for years – years of everything from 'That's not necessary' to 'That's really outside the scope of where we want to build this to', 'No, that actually belongs on the PM (project management) ladder', or 'That belongs on the strategy ladder.'

They basically told me I was unqualified to do what I was already doing. And I just found that infuriating, but super motivating. So, after three years of kicking against that glass ceiling, they finally relented. And what I also don't share in the book is I shared that very first title with a man. Paul was advocating for the exact same role but coming at it from the PM ladder, and they realized that Paul and I were pitching the same job description, and it was because both of us were coming at it that they actually opened their eyes and had that 'aha' moment of what this could give the company. Now it is pervasive throughout the company.

Anyone who has been an executive, who has been challenged to do something disruptive, has that right-hand partner that is the Chief of Staff. It was revolutionary within the company and quickly became standard practice within tech like wildfire after that. Now we are seeing other companies that want to do innovative things also recognizing and adopting this as a key part of being innovative and challenging the status quo.

I asked Ann for her advice for assistants that really want to take that step up into leadership. She said:

Start today. I find a lot of us pause and we wait until we have this perfect playbook plan where we are sure we are not going to fail, and we know where we are going. I don't think that is how any of this ever works; it certainly has not been for me.

Take a micro-bet on yourself right now. Write down your goals. Start with your mission, vision, and values for yourself, for your life, and realize the decisions you are making today are your living legacy. If the pandemic has taught us anything, it is that we cannot take for granted this one single precious life that we have. Don't wait for tomorrow. Don't wait for someone else to give you permission to do something outside of how people currently define you or, more importantly, how you define yourself. Write down your mission, vision and values and do things that are aligned with them. And start. Take a small sprint, a little bet that you can accomplish today, and allow that to give you the courage and the bravery to expand beyond that. But start today.

And finally, Barack Obama and his former Special Assistant, Reggie Love.

Reggie started out as a staff assistant. which is the lowest rung on the totem pole, one step up from an intern. He initially answered mail and calls and took constituents on tours of the Capitol and Senate buildings for about six months.

As fate would have it, a backup of mail had been found in some closet in another office building. Barack Obama had been getting mail at the US Senate before he was ever sworn in, and over 10,000 pieces of mail were sitting there. The confusion was that he gave this great speech in the fall of 2000, and they had the DNC in Boston during the John Kerry presidential campaign. He was also running for US Senate in the state of Illinois. And so this backlog of mail hadn't been opened, and it was really old. Reggie helped respond to all the mail, and learned that there were some resources that they could use. There was a scanning service and some FTP (file transfer protocol) sites that they took advantage of until they were able to devise a way to digitize it, allowing them to answer it more quickly.

Reggie says:

Pete Rouse who had hired me, nothing got him more excited than constituent services and mail. He felt like that was the pulse of understanding what was happening in the country. He thought I had turned water into wine by coming up with this process to answer mail more quickly. I told him there was a scanner in the basement, and there was this FTP site, and we had a couple of interns, so when Barack Obama decided to run for president, Pete thought, you can put Reggie anyplace, and he'll help solve problems.

He asked me what I wanted to do on the presidential campaign. I was 23 at the time, and I said, 'Why don't you just put me in a role that you think I'll be good at?' And so he said, 'Why don't you go on the road and handle stuff for the candidate? So, I became the body man. That's the person who's on the ground with the candidate, supporting them as they are moving through and trying to execute what are usually pretty hectic days, but also there to make sure that the candidate has everything they need. I think it's more applicable in politics, as you have more events held outside of the office: fundraisers, rallies, political events and interviews at different TV stations, for example.

People felt like anyone who had that job must've been from Chicago, or their parents must be donors, or there must have been some deep connection. But it just came down to the fact that Pete had trusted me.

There were probably two elements of it. I would always listen and ask pertinent questions that I think oftentimes may have shown some of my novice and insecurities. But rather than trying to stumble through something that I didn't have a lot of certainty on, I always made sure to ask clarifying questions about things that maybe I should have known. When I made mistakes, I really tried to own them. It's easy to say this wasn't my fault. And some things may not have directly been my fault, but I would often say, 'That wasn't great, and we've got to be better'. These were things that I think the President respected, and helped build trust between the two of us.

One day we were headed from Florida to South Carolina; his briefcase that had some debate prep notes was left in the back of the suburban, and when we landed in South Carolina, he asked 'Where's my bag?' At that moment, instead of making excuses, I just said 'It's my fault and it will never happen again'.

I lived about four blocks from the White House, and every day I would walk from my apartment across Lafayette Park at about 7 am. It felt like an immense amount of opportunity and blessing. I thought there were a lot of issues that someone like Barack Obama would be able to tackle. It felt like an immense opportunity to be a part of an administration that was able to help create equality for all people. But then also a lot of pressure, because as the first African American president I always felt like he carried this burden that he had to get it right. He didn't want to have any scandals and didn't want to be in a scenario where the country would look back and say we knew we should've never gone in that direction. And, even when things went wrong, the stories were never about me. They would always be about him or his administration.

I felt compelled to make sure none of my actions led to something that would bring additional scrutiny to his administration. I think he did a great job, and I think a lot of people felt that not only was it a monumental opportunity for the individuals that worked there, but it was a monumental opportunity for democracy and for the country.

I think it was an immense sort of education for me. What was at the beginning a national education around the campaign for the presidency became a global international education for me in terms of the impact the US and a president has, on so many other parts of the world. The first thing I did was put a map of Africa next to my desk, because I realized how many countries there were there. I really needed to figure out where they were and what the capitals were. Who are the presidents? Who were the Prime Ministers? What are their natural resources? What are the issues going on? That was a thing that I always felt myself having to learn because so many of those issues would come up in the daily briefings.

Interestingly, I have had the privilege of interviewing not only all three of the above but also the former assistants of Richard Branson, Princess Diana, Oprah Winfrey, JFK Junior, Bill Gates and Ronald Reagan.

When I asked each of them what advice they would give to a new assistant, every one of them immediately told me that no job was too small or insignificant. The job is one of servant leadership and that means rolling up your sleeves and doing whatever it takes to support your manager to make them the best that they can be.

If you buy into the premise that you are employed to maximize your manager's performance, this is a no-brainer.

Managing up is about adopting a proactive mindset. Where can you take on greater responsibility and add more value to your partnership? To be clear, I'm not talking about more work – I know you have plenty of that – but if AI is going to take much of the repetitive, task-based work, there is room to step into more strategic, proactive leadership of your manager's workload.

But that takes confident communication, which I believe is the key to an assistant's success.

Still wondering if you are a leader? Remember:

'Leadership is action, not position' – Donald H McGannon.

'Leadership is influence, nothing more, nothing less' – John Maxwell.

'If your actions inspire others to dream more, learn more, do more and become more, you are a leader' – John Quincy Adams.

CHAPTER FOUR

Communication, the key to advancement

When we run surveys for the magazine about what goes wrong in relationships between leaders and assistants, you could run one thread through every single response we get. It all boils down to communication and if you want to become a world-class assistant, becoming a confident and effective communicator is a must.

That means we need to think about our soft skills as well as the hard skills that we so often focus on:

- Are you aware not just of what you ask for but also how you ask for it?
- How open are you to learning?
- Are you curious? How are your questioning and listening skills?
- Are you self-aware?
- Are you sensitive to how your actions and behaviours affect others?
- Are you clear on what your values are?

Before we look at the practicalities of communication, understanding yourself is core. Why do you behave and think in certain ways? You need to understand the WHY before you get to grips with the HOW.

Communication is made up of three elements (Mehrabian and Weiner, 1967) and when you understand it, it's a revelation.

1 Your body language is responsible for a massive 55 per cent of your communication.
2 Your tone and pace and pitch of voice accounts for 38 per cent.
3 And surprisingly, words only make up 7 per cent.

It's why, if you have ever spent hours writing and re-writing an email because you want to make sure the tone is right, I have news for you. They will receive it in whichever mindset they are currently in. If you don't know what I am talking about, does Figure 4.1 say 'You matter. Don't give up' or 'You Don't Matter. Give up'?

FIGURE 4.1   How do you read this? Is your automatic perspective positive or negative?

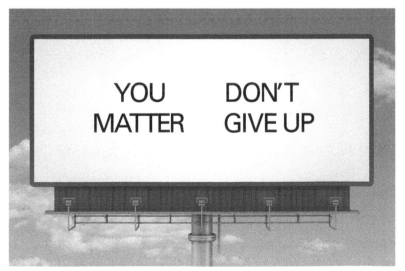

It's worth noting that if you are now working remotely, this is of utmost importance. I have seen many assistants get into hot water since the pandemic because they are only communicating by email or text message. Communication this way can take on a tone. Far better, as the stats above show, to either get face-to-face in person or online so you can see each other's body language. And if that won't work, pick up the phone. This will help you to avoid miscommunication.

Body language is a huge subject, and it can make an enormous difference in your being seen as a confident businessperson.

So, where does body language come into play here?

Firstly, understand what your body language is saying about you.

My husband says that he can tell when I am stressed because I play with my wedding ring. He calls it my worry bead. Or I might tap a pencil against my hand. Or I cross my legs and jiggle my foot. Whatever it is that I do, it's about the fact that stress produces energy that needs to go somewhere. It's a diversionary tactic used to distract ourselves and shows internal conflict to those watching us.

If you've seen the film *Pretty Woman*, you will remember the scene where Richard Gere has taken Julia Roberts to a polo match. She's wearing a gorgeous brown dress and stunning hat. He looks at her and says, 'You look beautiful. Don't fidget.'

This is an important piece of advice when it comes to being taken seriously, especially when you have something difficult or contentious that you want to say. Learn how to be still and say what you need to say.

Especially for women, they are often told that they are too emotional. I don't know about you but whenever I am furious or really nervous, my biological reaction is to go very red and often I can feel tears welling up. There is nothing worse. I feel it makes me look weak, when in fact I am just furious.

When I was appointed to a board for the first time, there was one particular man who took great delight in trying to get the women to cry. He was famous for it. If I was to be taken seriously, clearly something had to give. So, I went and got therapy and they gave me three pieces of advice that I still use to this day.

The first is to breathe. That might sound obvious but you know when you are feeling stressed and like you are losing your mind? You can't organize your thoughts properly. That is because, when you are stressed, your breathing becomes much shallower. This means your brain, quite literally, is not getting enough oxygen. So, stop. Take three deep breaths in and three breaths out – imagine it's a circular motion. By the time you get to the third breath, you will have enough oxygen to think clearly.

Secondly, take a glass of water in with you. When you become stressed, you swallow more, and this produces acid saliva which is what makes you feel sick. Not only that, but the action of drinking and swallowing relaxes you.

And thirdly, practice being able to say what you need to say without facial expressions or emotions whilst being able to look the other person directly in the eye when you say it. This is one of the most powerful tools I learned on my journey to senior management. It takes practice but after a while you will start to recognize what that state of calm feels like and you will be able to put yourself into it when you need to.

The other truly powerful tool is to understand what your posture and how you stand is saying about you.

When you stand with your hands hanging by your sides, it feels uncomfortable for you and also for people looking at you. Your arms feel too long for your body and you are not sure what to do with your hands. That's because in evolutionary terms, our arms ARE slightly orangutang at this point. But what should you do with them?

One option is crossed arms. But it suggests that you are putting up a barrier.

It's always interesting when I train people because I understand their body language. Usually, particularly when I am doing in-house training, there are at least a couple of people in the audience who have their arms crossed. It's like they are saying, 'They've told us you're good. Let's see, shall we? I reserve judgement.'

After about 10 minutes, the arms come down and they incline their heads. This is a sign that they now trust you and don't think you are going to try and bite them on the neck and kill them.

Then there is the hands on hips or 'Wonder Woman' pose.

When lizards are in danger and want to make themselves look more powerful, they puff out their heads to make themselves look bigger and scare their enemy away. Whether you are standing with one hand or both hands on your hips, that is exactly what you are doing. You are commanding the space and it's a power play.

In her TED Talk about body language, Amy Cuddy says that if you are feeling nervous about a meeting, you should go into a side room or a bathroom stall and stand in this power pose until you have released the endorphins you need. It's a great idea in theory, because it puts you into the correct posture to breathe properly, which helps with nerves, but I have to admit to having a giggle at the thought of people all over the world standing in bathrooms with their hands on their hips.

Men have a different way of adopting the lizard pose, which involves putting both hands behind their head to make themselves look bigger. This is often accompanied by manspreading legs.

Then there is the fig leaf gesture, with one hand placed on top of the other over the pelvis. It usually occurs when you feel vulnerable, and it's a natural instinct to try to cover your metaphorical nakedness. Like the crossed arms, it is putting up a barrier. The problem with using it is that it closes you in and hunches your shoulders. And exposing your vulnerability reduces perceptions of your strength.

Showing your palms is a symbol of trust. It shows you are not hiding anything in your hands. We often show our open palms when we ask people to trust us. So, when we have our hands in our pockets, it suggests that we have something to hide.

Here's a great tip for meetings.

Imagine a board room, with people sitting around a table. Now imagine that they all have their hands underneath the desk. They don't look very engaged, do they? And they look subservient. Now imagine the same room with everyone sitting with their arms over the table.

Instantly more engaged, aren't they?

A wise old businessman once told me that if I was sitting in a meeting and I wanted to say something, I should sit with the power triangle, when the hands are clasped together forming a triangle with the table. He said that if I sat like this, someone would always ask me what I wanted to say. I have used this technique for over 20 years, and although I have never been able to track down why, it works. Try it.

If you want to present yourself as being part of a meeting rather than someone who is there to 'support', make sure you are sitting with your hands above the table. If you don't want to say anything, simply keep your arms in the triangle and lower them.

As an aside, do you know the psychological effect when men wear suits? The V of the suit jacket lapels against the shirt is intended to make their shoulders look broader and therefore make them look more powerful.

And what is the effect of men wearing ties? It's to make sure that you focus on their face. This also makes them appear more powerful. It's why Steve Jobs was always photographed in a polo-necked jumper. You had to focus on his face. It's also why we associate women that wear chunky jewellery with being powerful. We focus on their face. It's a great tip if, as a woman, you have a large cleavage. Wearing chunky jewellery will help keep them focused on your face.

And finally, what about holding your hands behind your back?

It's very King Charles, isn't it? But standing like this means your posture is correct and that is important for the way that you are perceived.

Imagine for a minute that you need to walk into a meeting, to interrupt in order to relay an important message. You timidly knock on the door and scuttle into the room, looking nervous. There are people in every business that I call 'the scuttlers'. You know the people that I mean; the ones who scuttle around the office, hunched over, looking like they want to disappear into themselves. Their body language says they have no confidence in themselves. They would rather be invisible. You nervously tell the people in the meeting that you are sorry to interrupt but you have an important message for your manager.

Now imagine the same situation again, except for this time, before you knock on the door, you hold your thumb behind your back for three seconds to ensure you are standing in perfect posture, and you do your three deep breaths to ensure you are calm and comfortable. Now you walk confidently into the room and say, 'Please excuse the interruption but I have an important message for XXX'.

The impression is entirely different.

Be careful about the messages you are giving. What is your body language saying about you? If you are sat at your desk with your head in your hands or yawning, or you keep checking your watch, what impression do you think you are giving?

Likewise, smiling changes everything. Sometimes when I train this session, an assistant will say to me that they don't know how to change their expression – they 'just have one of those faces'. I don't understand this. If you know, and you understand how it changes people's perceptions of you negatively, it's worth making the effort to do something about it. We all know some-one in the office who is amazing at their job but also consistently grumpy and miserable. We would rather not deal with them, given a choice. Don't be that person.

A brief word about colour. There is a whole discussion for another time about the impact of colour psychologically, but I just want to say this. When I am on stage and looking out at an audience of assistants, I see a sea of black, beige, brown, dark green and other colours designed to make you fade into the background.

When I am headlining a conference, I will wear bright colours; I even had bright red and blue suits made in Hong Kong, specifically for when I am keynoting. I want people in the audience to be able to see me easily, wherever I am in the room. And I want the way I am dressed to say that I am confident and outgoing. If I am conducting an interview or emceeing a conference, I am usually in much more muted colours. I am not the focus. The other speakers and interviewees are.

Don't be scared to wear colour, even if it is just a splash. You'll be surprised at how it changes the way people see you.

There is work to do on understanding your signature gestures. If body language is responsible for 55 per cent of your communication, you can see how important it is to create a perception of yourself by understanding how your gestures, your posture and your demeanour define who you are before you even speak a word.

In fact, truly understanding yourself, your inner thinking, behaviours and value systems, is of huge importance. You need to understand yourself before you try to understand your leader.

Johari Window is a framework that I often use to help with this. It's particularly useful when working with teams that are in conflict, but it has to be handled carefully because in this context, it's about each person exploring how they see themselves and then the rest of the group talking about how THEY see them. But I'm not doing that today. I'm just using it as a way to get you thinking.

FIGURE 4.2   The Johari Window model

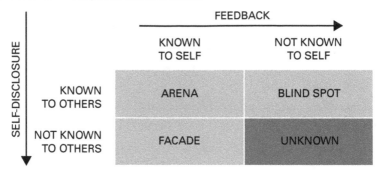

The premise is that there are four quadrants:

- **Arena,** which is the things you know about yourself and other people also know about you. This is how you behave when you are with people you know really well. Maybe friends or family. You feel comfortable being open and totally yourself.
- **Mask,** which is the things you know about yourself but other people may not know about you. This is how you behave when you want to hide certain things about yourself, maybe when you are with people that you don't know so well, perhaps in a work environment, for example.
- **Blind spot,** which is the things you don't know about yourself but other people know about you. A simple but good example of this is that recently we had a new member of staff start. As they walked her around the business and got to me, they introduced me but suggested she shouldn't talk to me before I had had my coffee as I was a nightmare. I laughed and said that I didn't think I was that bad. My entire team looked up and endorsed that yes, I was horrible before I had coffee. So now I know!!
- **Unknown,** which are the things you don't know about yourself and nobody else knows about you either – yet! This to me is the most exciting quadrant because it could be anything you want it to be. Anything at all.

Back in 2010, I was working for an international publishing company as a publishing director. I had 13 magazines, 80 staff and a huge budget to achieve. I was on a train at 7 am and was rarely home before 10 pm. Between us, my husband and I have seven children, it was year-end and we were in a recession.

For weeks I had been struggling. I was exhausted and can vividly remember sitting on buses and trains thinking, 'I can't do this today. I just need to go home and sleep.' But I continued to push myself because we had year-end to deliver. People kept asking me if I was OK and I assured them that I was. I think I was even fooling myself into thinking I was OK.

One day I walked into the office, and it was almost like my brain said, 'Well if you're not going to stop, I am going to stop you.' I had hundreds of things that I needed to do and I couldn't think of one of them. I had shut down mentally. It was terrifying. I told my manager I was going home and went straight to a doctor who diagnosed exhaustion and signed me off for five weeks with some very strong tablets. I slept.

Five weeks later, there was no job to return to. In my absence, they had restructured. It was the best thing they could have done for me. It forced me to get off the hamster wheel and look at what I really wanted to do with my life.

After a failed first marriage, the number of kids we had and huge outgoings, I had kept working flat out at a job I really wasn't happy in, to make sure the money kept coming in. I quickly discovered that we could adjust to less money coming in, and when I was happier, so was my family.

I looked for things I could do that weren't as pressured.

I had acquired a quarterly publication for assistants in 2003 called *Executive Secretary*. It had been run since 1989 by its founder, Jo Denby. She gifted it to me on the condition that I never put advertising in it, and that I continued to service the subscribers who had paid for it. After discussion with my husband, we agreed to try to launch it as a proper global magazine, but one that I could run from my kitchen table. Ironically, as it turns out, we saw it as a way to get a better work/life balance.

If you had told me then that it would have become a vehicle that would quite literally change the world for the administrative profession, that it would earn me an OBE, that I would speak in over 60 countries and headline at some of the biggest conferences in the world for assistants, or that I would count amongst my friends the assistants to Princess Diana, Bill Gates, Jeff Bezos, Oprah Winfrey, Barack Obama, JFK Junior, Sir Richard Branson, Archbishop Desmond Tutu and Nelson Mandela, I would clearly have thought that you were mad. And yet here I am.

That 'Unknown' quadrant has real power.

You need to turn understanding yourself into a fine art. The values that we hold dear will be different for each of us. Of course, we know we don't kill people and we don't steal but other things are less black and white. And how you feel about them is based on how you were brought up. What did your parents, your school, your place of worship teach you?

The things that you value about other people are usually the things that you value about yourself, and we are drawn to people who have the same values as we do. I usually find that when we get into conflict within our businesses and feel uncomfortable it's because either a person or the business itself does not align with our core values.

The entrepreneur Jeff Hoffman, whom I have mentioned already, has a wonderful session that I saw him present in New York called 'What if Saturday Never Comes?'. In it he talks about a friend of his, let's call him John, who was a bit of a daredevil. When Jeff first started in business, John would regularly call by the office trying to tempt Jeff into going abseiling or rally car driving or any number of other slightly dangerous activities. Jeff used to tell him, 'Maybe on Saturday'.

One day, John was killed in pursuit of one of these activities.

At his funeral, Jeff realized the impact that John had had on those in his life. The mourners talked at length about what John had done for them and for the community. It made Jeff think hard about what his legacy would be if he died. And he realized it would be that he had made a lot of money – and that wasn't enough. If you look for Jeff on LinkedIn, you will see that he now travels across the world teaching entrepreneurship, particularly in developing nations.

Hearing his presentation had a profound impact on me. It made me question what my values were and what I wanted my legacy to be. It's one of the reasons that I accepted when approached to become a director of the Isipho charity in South Africa. We take young adults who have few opportunities in life and give them a year's training in administration. And then we try to find them work.

But back to values. Are you clear on what your values are and what you want your legacy to be? Because I'm pretty sure it's not 'They were amazing at filing'.

Jeff Bezos is widely quoted as saying that your personal brand is what people say about you when you are not in the room. What do you want them to be saying about you?

How we show up is all about mindset. Assistants build cultures within their businesses, and you can change the entire energy in the office. You'd better be sure it's in a good way.

I once went to a Liza Minnelli concert at the London Palladium. We were lucky enough to be sitting in a box, which meant that we could see her standing in the wings waiting to go on. She was hunched over like an old woman, puffing on a cigarette and sipping on what looked like a large scotch.

And then the lights went down and the voice of god announced, 'Ladies and Gentlemen, Miss Liza Minnelli'. And she pulled herself up to her full height, stubbed out her cigarette and downed her scotch, and then she grabbed the man standing next to her and kissed him full on the lips before walking out on stage and delivering a spectacular two-hour performance.

But don't we all do a version of that every day?

There are days when I step into the elevator in the morning, and I have been dealing with a problem with one of my children, or the car has broken down, or I've had a disagreement with someone. But when those doors open, I walk out and wish everyone a cheery good morning. Why? Because that's the job, isn't it? And especially as an assistant, if you don't put on your mask, the rest of the staff worry that there is a problem.

We're going to talk about personalities now. Let me tee it up for you. In London, there are numerous awards for assistants, and there was one assistant who won lots of them during this particular year. And then, one day, she called me in tears. Her previous leader had left, and she had a new one. She told me that she was doubting her own abilities. Maybe she was just an amazing assistant to the last leader. She felt the new one hated her. So, we went for a gin and tonic, as you do in London, and talked it through. It turned out that the first leader was one type of personality and the new one was the polar opposite. We talked about how she might manage the new one, and she went back and implemented what we had talked about, and hallelujah, all was right in the world again.

In his book *The 7 Habits of Highly Effective People* (1990), Stephen Covey says, 'You treat them the same by treating them differently', and this is particularly important in your role. You might be looking after several managers, and you might have one of them that you absolutely love, maybe there are a couple that you think are OK, and if you're unlucky you might have one that when you meet them in the corridor, you're like a couple of cats; your back goes up and you want to hiss. But you are paid to treat them all the same, no matter how you feel about them.

Let's take a look at a difference model. Can you see where your manager sits?

Red: The Red is very similar to the Shaper in Belbin. They are parental in style and have a strong desire to win. They are not scared to make decisions, whether they upset people or not. They are driven and quick to challenge. If you present them with a one-pager with 10 bullet points on it, they are probably bored before they get to the third bullet point. They're insensitive, easily bored, ruthless and make up their mind quickly – often without all the information.

Yellow: The Yellow is very similar to the Resource Investigator in Belbin. They are charismatic and people-focused. People love to follow them because they are direct and open. They are fun-loving and trusting of others. They have the ability to make others feel welcomed and included. However, they are also horrible timekeepers, undisciplined, impulsive and disorganized.

Green: The Greens are great listeners, loyal, dependable, nurturing and passive. You can't rush them. If you try to get them to decide things too quickly, you will scare them. They are easily influenced, cautious, submissive, rely on outside approval, hate change and are slow to trust.

Blue: The Blue follows the rules. They make great numbers or analytics or quality control people. They are exceptionally well organized and analytical and have high expectations. But they are fiercely slow to make decisions, they procrastinate like mad, are closed to new ideas and need evidence before they decide to do anything.

Most of us are all four colours – I am Red/Yellow (depending on what kind of day I am having), then Green, and my Blue is almost non-existent. But that's why I employ Fran to fill that gap. Some businesses have Lego bricks on each desk with the colours in the order in which the occupant likes to be communicated with. What a great idea!

But before I talk more about the best way to communicate with each personality type, I want to explore micromanagement and the Blue personality.

For any employee, micromanagement is frustrating. When a manager keeps checking up on us and won't let us get on with the job, we instinctively feel that we are not trusted and it's uncomfortable. But often, they are just Blue.

My husband is Blue. I have to tell you that I had him do the Belbin assessment before I married him – only because I was about to teach it for the first time – but understanding who he is and what makes him tick has been very useful over the last 25 years.

There was a three-week speaking tour of the United States that I was due to go on, just before Covid-19. I was in a different city almost every night, so as you can imagine the schedule was quite complex. The night before I was due to travel, and you know how hectic it is the night before a trip, my husband decided that he needed to go through the schedule with me. It didn't matter how much I protested that the schedule was already in the calendar, he headed off to get his book to write it all down.

So, we started at the beginning. Which taxi firm was coming to collect me, at what time, and they were taking me to which airport and which terminal, and did I have the flight number and which airline was it and what time would I arrive and who was collecting me at the other end and did I have a number for them, and which hotel was I staying in, and which client was it? Oh my goodness! This was just the first city in a three-week trip!

Eventually, we got through it. He shut the book and I resumed my packing. I suspect he never looked at the information again. It's a good thing that I know he is Blue and not just trying to drive me mad. Does he trust me? Of course. Implicitly. But he needed the information to feel comfortable.

Going back to my friend, the award-winning assistant. Her manager had previously been a Red, so she was used to going in on a Friday with a list of bullet points explaining what she had been doing and what she would be doing the next week.

The new one was Blue and so because the assistant was not providing detail, she thought that she didn't know what she was doing. A quick change in communication style and a much more in-depth report every week, and suddenly she was being seen as exceptional again.

My last word on the Blues. I recently had an assistant tell me in a course that they were going to have to leave their job because their manager was so awful. When I enquired why, she told me that she had broken her leg, and when she called to tell him, he didn't ask how she was; instead, he asked when she was likely to be back. She was really upset. However, I explained that he was simply being Blue. Blues don't think in emotions; they think in facts. So when she called, of course, his first thought was how long she would be off. He wasn't a bad person; he was just being Blue.

Let's look now at how you should communicate with each colour by revisiting the 55 per cent body language, 38 per cent tone, pace and pitch of voice, and 7 per cent words that make up your communication style.

Figure 4.3 shows the body language you should adopt for each colour, the tone you should be speaking in, and the kinds of words and phrases you should be using.

As you can see, the Reds are all about strength and decisiveness. There is nothing that a Red hates more than someone a bit weak and watery. They are not scared to say it exactly as it is, even if it risks upsetting someone, and they respect those that stand up to them.

Can you see how by understanding the above, you will be able to work far more effectively with your manager? So, in which order, by colour, does your manager like to be communicated with?

Once you understand that, the way you provide information to them and the way that you communicate with them will

FIGURE 4.3 Different personalities and how to communicate with them

	RED	YELLOW	GREEN	BLUE
55% Body language	Keep your distance Strong handshake Lean forward Direct eye contact Controlled gestures	Get close Use touch Fun Friendly eye contact Expressive gestures	Relaxed, closed Methodical Lean back Friendly eye contact Small gestures	Keep your distance Stand or sit Firm posture Direct eye contact No gestures
38% Tone, pace and pitch of voice	Strong Clear, loud Confident Direct	Enthusiastic High and low modulation Friendly Energized	Warm Soft Steady Low in volume	Clear Precise Limited inflection
7% Words and comment	Win Lead the field Results Now Challenge	Fun I feel Socialize Recognition Exciting	Step by step Help me out Security Promise Think about it	Here are the facts It's been proven No risk Analyse Guarantee

change forever. I find that when I meet someone now, after a few moments I have worked out what colour they are. And this not only changes the way in which I communicate with them, but it can also have a positive effect on our relationship. Things that I would once have taken personally are no longer catalysts for conflict. They are simply personality traits.

A great example of this is my Senior Editor, Kathleen Drum. She is a superb editor and does a great job but she is a Blue. In the beginning we clashed terribly. I can remember one occasion in particular where I had spent three months working on a new website. When it launched I was thrilled with it and couldn't wait to share it with the team. However, I was also exhausted from putting lots of hours in, so when I sent it out to the team with a great flourish, and the first response I got was, 'There's a comma missing on line three', I have to admit to being tearful and explosive. I took it terribly personally. I believe I may even have said something along the lines of, 'Do you think you might say just one positive thing before you start looking at what's wrong with it?' Oversensitive? Certainly.

But these days, now she has done my course, we get on like a house on fire. In fact, we will joke with each other. I'll tell her to stop being so Blue. And she'll comment that something I just did was particularly Yellow.

Understanding these different personalities and how to communicate with each other is one of the keys to successful partnership and to leading up.

Reference

Mehrabian, A and Weiner, M (1967) Decoding of inconsistent communications, *Journal of Personality and Social Psychology*, **6** (1), pp 109–14

CHAPTER FIVE

Quality conversations, office politics and emotional intelligence

In the perfect scenario, when you are having a conversation with someone, you will be telling the other person something. And the other person will be listening with the intention of understanding. This is called active listening, and it's much harder than it sounds because most people don't listen properly. They are too busy thinking about how they are going to respond. This causes problems because when we don't properly hear what is said, we misunderstand or misinterpret things. And this causes conflict. In most cases we don't fight because we disagree. We fight because we fail to understand.

I want to talk to you for a moment about Transactional Analysis, or TA.

Have you ever found yourself in a situation with someone where you are repeating the same uncomfortable patterns with them every time you interact? For example, maybe they are always trying to get you to say yes to taking on their work?

Or they talk over you when you have something you really want to say. Maybe they make you feel lesser than them. Or jumpy because you know they are not going to let you express yourself. Perhaps they are always critical of how you handle things.

Transactional analysis is a theoretical framework which says that it's not the other person's behaviour that causes the problem. It's our own state of mind.

Developed in the 1960s by Eric Berne, it maintains that people communicate from one of three ego states: Parent, Adult or Child.

The Parent and Child ego states are divided into Parent: Nurturing or Aggressive – and Child: Rebellious or Passive.

The Parent Aggressive ego state is non-compromising. Think of how a parent speaks to a young child. For example, 'I told you it's time for bed. No arguments. Off you go.'

How does being spoken to like that as an adult make you feel? Disempowered? Disrespected? Not listened to?

Often we will see those on the receiving end of this communication style revert to a very childlike demeanour. Maybe they stammer or whisper or lower their eyes. They become a Child Passive, and this means they are compliant to the Parent's instructions rather than their own needs.

It's worth noting that where I see assistants behaving in the manner of the Parent Aggressive, when we explore it in more detail, it's usually because they have had a manager who behaved that way and so they think this is what leadership looks like. But if you are behaving this way, please recognize how it makes the other person feel and what their reaction is.

The other type of Parent is the Parent Nurturing ego state. These Parents want everyone to be happy and will go to great lengths to take care of everyone.

Often the reaction to those on the receiving end of a Parent Nurturing is that they lack discipline and behave however they want. They become a Child Rebellious. The result is that a business or department can quickly become unruly because the Child

Rebellious is entirely concerned with their own needs, rather than the needs of others or of the business.

Clearly, none of these ego states are where we want to be. They are unstable, disruptive and encourage a toxic environment. Where we want to aim for is the Adult Assertive ego state.

The Adult is not subdivided. That is because it operates in the here and now and takes on board all the information to make clear decisions. They deal with facts, not feelings and emotions. The typical Adult behaviours are being calm, rational, analytical, unemotional, logical and reasonable.

What has this got to do with you and your manager? Well, ideally, to maximize the partnership potential, you (and in the best-case scenario, your manager) need to be in the Adult Assertive ego state. It ties back into Belbin, collaboration, and the respect and trust piece. In the past, the role has been seen as one where the manager is the parent and the assistant is the child. The most successful partnerships understand that this is no longer the case.

Let's go back to our four colours and their personalities. Where do they sit when it comes to Transactional Analysis?

Well, our Reds are clearly parent aggressive in style, aren't they? They are argumentative, blameless and never wrong. What about our Greens? They are subdivided between Nurturing Parent, who overcompensates and creates rebellious children, or Passive Child. Our Yellows are very definitely children: undisciplined, needing to be managed to within an inch of their life and wanting to be liked. So where does that leave our Blues? They, of course, are adults. They want all the information before they make a decision.

Once we understand this, the need to actively listen to the other person becomes clear.

Have you ever played the game Chinese Whispers? The concept is that you tell one person a story or read them a short paragraph. They then tell that same story to person number two, who in turn relates it to person number three. By the time it gets to person number four relaying the story back to the entire group, it has often changed beyond recognition. Usually it has been distilled to a couple of lines. Facts and figures are either missed entirely, confused or just plain wrong. And this is when they have been told to listen. In 2014, researchers at the University of Iowa found that when it comes to memory, we don't remember things we hear nearly as well as things we see or touch (Bigelow and Poremba, 2014). Students' memory declined across the board when time delays grew longer, and the decline was much greater for sounds, and began as early as four to eight seconds after being exposed to them.

While this seems like a short time span, it's akin to forgetting a phone number that wasn't written down, says Poremba, one of the researchers: 'If someone gives you a number, and you dial it right away, you are usually fine. But do anything in between, and the odds are you will have forgotten it,' she says.

It's why you can sometimes sit in a meeting and later, when you hear a colleague relaying back what happened in that meeting, you think, 'Were we in the same meeting?' They are not telling lies. They simply haven't heard it and therefore remembered it in the same way as you have. Never rely on yourself to remember. Always take notes.

Getting back to having conversations with others and active listening, what are some ways that you can show that you are listening? You need to show the speaker that they are your focus and you are paying attention. In his 2015 book *Simple Reminders: Inspiration for living your best life*, Bryant McGill says, 'One of the most sincere forms of respect is actually listening to what another has to say.'

Firstly, get rid of distractions, particularly technology. I spend hours at my computer working. If someone interrupts me, I find it hard not to get cross or to come away from the work that I am doing to pay them the attention that they need. I have to consciously do it. And yet, I have been on the receiving end of that treatment. How do you feel when your manager doesn't look up from their screen when you go to talk to them and continues to type? Not great, right?

The best manager that I ever had used to shut his computer and move it, and the pile of papers in front of him, to one side whenever someone went in to have a meeting with him. It was his way of saying, 'You have my complete attention'. The loyalty and trust that he enjoyed from the whole team was in no small part down to this. He showed every member of his team this same courtesy and that he respected both their time and what they had to say to him. Powerful stuff!

Next, I would be conscious of the other person's body language. In the previous chapter, I talked a lot about how to make sure that your own body language is sending the messages that you want it to. But what about what other people's body language is telling you? And pay attention to their tone. For example, if they are telling you they are fine, but they are not smiling and their shoulders are slumped, chances are that they aren't alright at all.

Then you can nod, or smile and be open and inviting. Pay attention – this is not a competition. How annoying is it when someone asks you a question and before you have finished answering, they are talking over you because they are excited or think they have something important to say. The insinuation is that what they have to say is more important than what you are trying to share.

In another quote from *The 7 Habits of Highly Effective People: Powerful lessons in personal change*, Stephen Covey says, 'Most people don't listen with the intent to understand, they listen with the intent to reply.'

Show you're listening by giving sincere verbal affirmations and give simple feedback. For example, 'that's really interesting' or 'that's really useful to know'.

And ask clarifying questions. Make sure you truly understand. Right at the start of my career I worked in sales and I have never forgotten that when it came to understanding how to overcome objections the trick was to ask lots of questions until you got to the crux of the matter, before you tried to answer. For example, if a client told you something was too expensive, it could mean many things. It might mean, I don't see the value in it. Or it might mean, I am in the middle of working on something and don't want to talk to you right now. Or it could mean, I haven't got enough money to do this right now, or I have to talk to someone else before I make a decision. Do you see what I am saying? Unless you dig, you are never going to win because you could be answering an entirely different problem to the one that they have expressed on the surface.

So you've listened to understand and you've become skilled at reading situations by actively listening. But what happens when office politics raises its ugly head and it all becomes far more complicated?

I hate office politics with a passion. It's such a waste of time and energy, and it makes the person on the receiving end feel absolutely terrible. I've been known to threaten to fire people who are particularly playing games and causing angst. However, I am not stupid, so I know that it is a part and parcel of office life. As an assistant, you need to understand it, not least because your job is not to be afraid OF your executive. It's to be afraid FOR them. To do that, you need to understand how politics works in your office.

Where is the power? Who are the influencers? Who are particularly adept at deflecting blame when they get it wrong? And who is your executive? Are they a particularly political animal?

One of the best ways to identify the different political styles and motivations of those around you is to look at the animal model developed by Simon Baddeley and Kim James, as shown in Figure 5.1. I first became aware of it when I attended the late Susie Barron-Stubley's PA retreat in 2013. I love the simplicity of this model, not least because when I bump into former attendees of my training, they often tell me that this model was particularly useful when faced with a fox. It helped them to remember how to deal with it.

FIGURE 5.1   The animal model

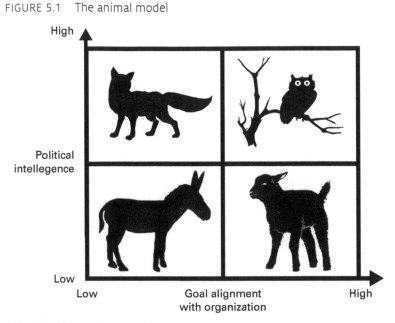

SOURCE Baddeley and James, 1987

Let's look at each animal then.

As you can see from the diagram, the fox is highly political but hasn't got an awful lot of interest in the success of the organization or the other people that they work with. They are likely to use their political skills for personal gain and are adept at manoeuvring and manipulating when backed into a corner to ensure that others take the blame.

The owl, on the other hand, might be equally politically aware but they are far more aligned with serving the needs of the business and the people that work in it. They are unlikely to use their political skills for personal gain. Instead, the owl's understanding of the political landscape and what is really going on is a means to keeping the status quo balanced, because their negotiation skills and understanding of what is really going on mean the kind of behaviour displayed by the fox doesn't gather any momentum. The owl is politically sophisticated but also has integrity.

Then there is the sheep. And our poor sheep are horribly naive. They stay away from politics because it scares them to death. They associate it with the fox's negative traits rather than the owl's positive ones. The problem is that, as Plato said, 'One of the penalties for refusing to participate in politics is that you end up being governed by your inferiors.' The result for the sheep is that they often end up getting the blame for things that they shouldn't because the fox will target them, knowing they are unlikely to stand up for themselves, because they don't know how the game is played.

And finally, there is the mule. The mule doesn't care about political games and doesn't really care about the business either. It's all about them and what they want and need. They're totally unaware of both formal and informal power structures and nor are they interested in getting involved in them. They are determined to stick resolutely to how they want to do things and are convinced that they are right in the way that they deal with things.

So which are you? What about your manager? And how about other colleagues or members of the leadership team that you regularly interact with?

If you are going to become a stronger, more effective assistant it is crucial to learn how to deal with office politics. Not just in terms of which animal traits those around you display, but also understanding how to get things done. What is the decision-making process? Who has the final word? And what happens during times of stress or uncertainty? Where does the power sit then?

How you react in these situations is closely linked to empathy, emotional intelligence and allowing the other person to save face, whilst not taking the blame for something you didn't do.

Going back to Transactional Analysis, it's about remaining firmly in the Adult ego state. You need to understand how it works in order to build your influence, and you can't become a high performer without learning to do so.

It helps to first understand the difference between culture and climate. Culture is how we do things at our organization, whereas climate is how we feel about how we do things at our organization. I have seen some hugely talented people, who love what they do, leave because they don't like how we are allowed to behave towards each other.

Let me give you an example of foxlike behaviour and how to deal with it.

A manager from another part of the business has asked for your help in securing a venue for a summer party later in the year. They mentioned it in passing at a meeting a couple of weeks ago, and you said you would be delighted to take a look for them, assuming they had asked because you have organized similar things in the past and are good at it. You suggested they drop you a line with more details, and you would come back to them. They have sent nothing. The only thing you have (possibly) done wrong is not to have proactively followed up on that conversation.

You receive the following email:

> I am surprised and disappointed that despite your agreeing to help with sourcing a venue for the summer party later this year, I have yet to receive any information. We are on a very tight deadline and I was expecting some ideas by the end of last week. It will be impossible to collate the budget in time for the management meeting now. Please give this your immediate attention and forward me suggestions by end of play today.

As you read it, you notice it has been copied to your manager and to the CEO.

Firstly, it's worth noting the reasons it has been sent by email rather than the manager calling you. It leaves a paper trail, it allows them to be a keyboard warrior and it presents the 'facts' in a way that manipulates the situation to make it look like it's all your fault.

It's a prime example of why office politics are so destructive. I don't know about you, but when I receive an email like this, I see red. I can't concentrate on anything else until I have put right the wrong that has been inflicted on me. And I will spend inordinate amounts of time composing a reply. I will be angry, upset and occasionally tearful.

And then a friend will ask me what's wrong. I will invite them to join me in composing a response. We will work hard to make sure it isn't too aggressive or too weak but once it's finally composed, it will probably be placed in a file until I have calmed down enough to make sure I haven't said anything I shouldn't have before I send it.

In the meantime, my friend has now gone to the water cooler, where another colleague asks if I am OK. The response? Oh my goodness, no, she isn't. You should see the email the fox sent her! All of a sudden the whole office is involved. No work is getting done. And the moment you press send with your response, the whole process will begin again at the other end.

What an enormous waste of time, money and energy!

Let's look at better ways to deal with it and how each of the animals might respond.

If I was a fox, I would seek to wound their reputation like they had wounded mine, so I would copy the manager and the CEO. My response would look something like this: 'I have been extremely busy with my day-to-day role and you didn't specify what your deadline was. I believe you might want to find someone else to help you with this.'

The problem with this answer is that it doesn't solve the problem. It's also relatively aggressive and will probably generate an equally angry response from the fox at the other end, so you will end up in a game of email tennis.

Let's look then at the mule. The mule believes that attack is the best form of defence and so their email response, copied to all, is likely to look something like this: 'This is not my responsibility – it's yours. You asked me to help and I was waiting for more details. I suggest you find someone else to help you as I am no longer interested in doing so.'

Of course, this is a really bad way to respond. It's thoroughly unprofessional, even if factually it is correct, and it's likely to send the whole situation stratospheric.

Our poor sheep is scared to death and certainly won't copy anyone in because they want as few people as possible to know that they failed. They probably won't sleep because they are so stressed by the whole situation. It's clear how they will respond: 'I am so sorry! I totally dropped the ball on this one. Let me look at it right now and I will come back to you immediately with some suggestions.'

The problem with this is that it wasn't the sheep's fault. By taking the blame, they are setting up future situations where the fox feels able to scapegoat the sheep when it suits them. Apart from which, we all have our own schedules and work to get through. By agreeing to do this immediately, the sheep has thrown their own workload out of the window in order to pander to the tantrums of the fox. Finally, saying sorry in a work setting is never as strong as saying 'I apologize'. That's much stronger.

It's time to look at how the owl would respond, and the response is a thing of beauty:

> I can see that you are upset, and I understand that you need to pull together some suggestions in time for the meeting. I apologize for not following up after our meeting, but was under the impression that you were going to forward me some further details before I made recommendations. If you would like to do that now, I would

be delighted to plan some research into my workflow so that I can get some suggestions to you before the end of the week.

So the owl takes control of the situation and resolves it but in an assertive way. Let's look at how they did that. Firstly, they use empathy in the first sentence by recognizing that the fox is upset and clarifying what it is that they need. Then they apologize. Note that they are not apologizing for what they are accused of, but rather for not following up, which is the only thing that they might have done wrong. They have very politely pointed out that there may have been a lack of communication without accusing the fox of anything. And they then suggest a resolution.

This is certainly an adult response, as opposed to the other three who are acting as parents and children.

The owl is definitely where we need to aspire to be.

We've talked a bit about emotional intelligence and why it's such an important part of being an assistant, but what is it?

Emotional intelligence (EI), also often referred to as emotional quotient or EQ, is the ability to manage both your own emotions and understand the emotions of people around you. There are five key elements to EI: self-awareness, self-regulation, motivation, empathy and social skills.

Back in 2015, we commissioned a psychological study in association with Avery UK which revealed marked differences in the abilities, experiences and personalities of assistants and their colleagues in the office (Lill, 2015). The study, which compared assistants with the rest of the UK working population, uncovered a number of extraordinary findings.

We looked at numerous factors of working life, including personality traits, stress levels and responsibilities, as well as their IQ, qualifications and emotional intelligence levels, comparing each aspect to the rest of the working population. The results, particularly around EQ, were striking. An assistant's EQ was 10 per cent higher than that of a normal office worker.

So where does EQ come into play for an assistant?

EQ ties into the value systems that we talked about earlier in the book. Our ethics, morals, principles and values tap into our subconscious and mean something different to each of us. To excel as an assistant, we need to be self-aware enough to understand how these things shape our behaviours. It's a strange career. Our success depends on our ability to serve others in such a way that they feel both served and led at the same time. We can't do this without a huge amount of emotional intelligence.

We also all have hot buttons that we need to be aware of, that are triggered by past experiences. Our inner drivers are often hidden from our consciousness so it needs considering. For example, you may have experienced workplace bullying in the past, and have come out the other end. Maybe you have changed jobs. But the first time someone raises their voice or treats you with disrespect, you immediately think, 'Here we go again'. It may not be the case at all, but all our experiences tell us that this is what is going on.

One of my pet hot buttons is taxi drivers. As you know, I travel a lot, and whenever I land at an airport and climb into a taxi, the first question they always ask me is, 'Have you ever been here before?' And my antennae go up. I am on high alert. My answer? 'Yes, many, many times.' This is in reaction to various taxi drivers over the last 12 years who have driven me halfway around the world in order to get a higher fare. Most are probably just making polite conversation. But my past experiences drive my reactions.

Whilst assistants are wonderful at reading other people and adapting to their personalities, what they are not so good at is pushing themselves forward. Because of the historical view of the role as one of 'support', and the way some businesses still view their administrative staff, many assistants are reluctant to step into the limelight. We need to stop living in the past. Twenty years ago this may have been a subservient role. But this is far from what the modern assistant role is. It's a partnership. An assistant is an administrative business partner, and as we have already determined, this opens up opportunities – but only if you take them.

The late Susie Barron-Stubley, a top international trainer, gave a wonderful example of how not using emotional intelligence can play out. Imagine for a moment that your manager is suddenly summoned to an important offsite meeting with a client on the day that they are due to present to the board about a project they have been working on for months. They ask you to attend the board meeting to present the project on their behalf.

What is your reaction?

It's all about perspective. For some of you, this would be your idea of hell.

After death, the thing most of us fear more than anything else is public speaking. As someone who has spoken all over the world to audiences as large as 3,000 people, I am here to tell you that it doesn't matter how many times I do it, or how many people are in the audience, I still feel physically sick about 10 minutes before I go on. Once I'm up there I am fine, but the day that I cease to feel this way is the day I should go home and not do it anymore, because the reason I feel this way is because it matters. I have realized that if I take the way I feel and use that energy, it makes for a better presentation.

You might be terrified of public speaking, but you would be nervous about speaking to the board, about whether you'd represent the project properly and about the fact that there has been very little preparation time. You present badly, you feel embarrassed and your worst fears are confirmed.

The alternative is that you are excited by the opportunity – you can see that speaking to the board shows your manager trusts you with such an important project. You put in some work to make sure you really understand the presentation – maybe you have a call with your manager to ask about anything you are unsure about. You present confidently and everyone is impressed.

The only difference in the two scenarios is your attitude. You need to be mindful of not jumping over opportunities simply because your head is telling you stories. Don't let your brain convince you that you can't do it. The amygdala – the part of your mind that is responsible for your fight or flight responses – might tell you to run away, that things are not possible. Your amygdala makes decisions a full seven seconds faster than your conscious mind. It's why we are often told to count to 10.

So next time someone asks you to do something and your response is fear, count to 10 before you decide. You don't want to jump over opportunities because you haven't thought it through properly.

References

Baddeley, S and James, K (1987) Owl, fox, donkey or sheep: Political skills for managers, *Management Learning*, **18** (1)

Bigelow, J and Poremba, A (2012) Achilles' Ear? Inferior human short-term and recognition memory in the auditory modality, *PLoS ONE*, **9** (2)

Lill, D (2015) Why PAs are your most valuable employees, Talk Business, https://www.talk-business.co.uk/2015/07/16/why-pas-are-your-most-valuable-employees/ (archived at https://perma.cc/MR8T-FS8Z)

CHAPTER SIX

Building powerful partnerships

When you start working with a manager for the first time, getting to know them and building that relationship takes time, and it's very definitely a process. It doesn't matter whether you have been an assistant for five minutes or for 30 years, the process is the same. And it helps to understand that it is a process.

Tuckman explained it best in his Model of Team Development (1965):

FIGURE 6.1 Tuckman's Model of Team Development

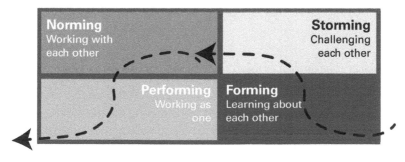

If you've ever seen the TV programme *Big Brother*, the process follows a similar path. When the housemates first enter the house, they are polite and excited to be there. But after a couple of days, the tension starts. They are working out each other's personalities and some of those personalities clash. They have different ideas on how they want to do things – particularly the challenges set. They find living together stressful and sometimes irritating. And then, somehow, they work it out. They figure out how to work together most effectively. In most cases by the end of the season there are strong bonds made and the housemates work well together to achieve the challenges.

The same is true when you are onboarding with a new executive. At the start, you both play nicely. It's polite and structured so that you both work through the first few weeks to set up or learn new systems and processes and get to know each other on a surface level. This is the FORMING quadrant.

But then the trouble starts as you move into STORMING. This quadrant can be anything from gently disagreeing to all-out war. You are both trying to establish the way you want to work and what expectations are. Because you now know each other a bit, you are pushing boundaries and working through what you want to change or improve.

I have had people on my course tell me afterwards that they feel they have spent five years in this storming phase and that it's so helpful to understand that it is just a process. They now understand it isn't personal and that they just have to push out of the other side to NORMING.

The NORMING phase is where you have both established how it's going to work and are working confidently with each other.

But where you really want to be is in the final phase – the PERFORMING quadrant. When you reach this point, you have got to the holy grail of assistant/manager partnership that I talked about earlier in the book, where one of you breathes in and the other breathes out. You have reached the status of true partners. The two of you have become one perfect employee for the business by taking the two very different skill sets that you possess and working together so seamlessly that you are now two sides of one coin.

It's worth noting that it takes time to get to the PERFORMING quadrant. Assistants often write to me because they are worried that the trust element is not there in their relationship with their executive. When I ask them how long they have been working together, typically it's under 18 months. The minimum amount of time it takes to properly build the partnership is 18 months in my opinion, so if you aren't there yet, don't fret. You are simply just still going through the process.

When you get a new manager, you are always going to be reactive and subordinate, but as you become more involved, you gain in confidence, which makes you more assertive. You feel able to offer your own ideas and insights until eventually you get to the point where there is structured communication, and you enter into a collaborative partnership.

You should also be aware that you aren't necessarily going to be at the PERFORMING quadrant with every aspect of your role even then. My current EA has been in the role for over two years but during that time we haven't run any of our live events because of Covid-19, so although she is very definitely PERFORMING beautifully in most areas, we are still in STORMING with our live events piece because it's a new part of the role.

But what happens if you have more than one manager?

For more than a century, assistants would have expected to work with just one manager, but that is no longer the case. Assistants all over the world are being asked to look after more than one manager and many are looking after teams too. And most are unhappy about it. The media doesn't help with this misrepresentation of how it works, perpetuating the myth that the assistant/manager relationship is exclusive.

In fact, our latest statistics paint a very different picture. Almost half of all assistants are managing four managers or more, and it's only one in five that have that 1:1 partnership relationship. It all depends on how your business is structured. More often than not, the model that I am seeing adopted is one where those in the C-suite get that 1:1 support from a level 4 assistant, the next level of management get 1:3–4 from either a level 4 or a level 3 assistant, and the lower levels have access to a pool of level 1–2 assistants who purely do reactive, administrative tasks.

And of course, it's cyclical. What tends to happen is that organizations decide that 1:1 support is vanity on the part of those supported, so they move to a model where the assistants have multiple managers to support. Then after a few years, they realize that this is making their managers less effective and productivity is affected, so they move back to the 1:1 model. When an organization understands how to calculate each of their administrative professionals' worth based on the hours they save their manager, it becomes a no-brainer. Does it for example make sense for a manager to be doing their own expenses? Strictly speaking, these types of tasks should be delegated to someone being paid a lesser rate per hour. It's simple economics. Doing the maths will help your organization to understand what assistant–manager ratio you need.

The problem with managing multiple managers is that if you get it wrong, you can end up jeopardizing not only your career but theirs too. Working for too many managers can cause burnout because you are overloaded with work. In addition, the more managers you have, the more conflicting messages you are likely to get, and some managers want to feel like they are the most important person you work with, so the politics around that can be a minefield. How do you prioritize what you need to do when everyone is shouting at once?

A word to the wise. If you find yourself in this situation, get them to talk to each other and decide what their priorities are.

This situation is a little like warring parents. It isn't your responsibility, but you will end up getting hurt and whether deliberately or not, it will suit them to have you stuck in the middle. Tell them you need them to work out the priorities and let you know, otherwise you will find yourself in the wrong and being blamed for things not getting done.

The best way to manage multiple managers is to provide visibility to all parties on what you are working on, and what your workload currently looks like.

It's hard to communicate how much you have on your plate and manage expectations with multiple people, but we very quickly worked out a great system for doing this.

It's called Timeboxing and essentially what it means is that everything my assistant is working on goes into her calendar. Not just meetings, but everything. So she not only handles my calendar but also has her own. Into that, she puts all the things she is working on currently.

I hate to-do lists with a passion. They are like Medusa. You cut one head off and five more grow back. They are deeply depressing because you never feel you have achieved what you should have done. Timeboxing allows you to timeline the tasks and projects you are working on so you know you have completed what you needed to do today.

Using Timeboxing, Fran decides what her priorities are and adds them to the calendar, along with meetings and specific times for dealing with email (we'll come onto that later).

We all have visibility of that calendar. And I can see where there are gaps if I need anything done urgently. If you have multiple managers, this is particularly helpful because your workload then becomes clear to everyone and you can better manage expectations.

If your manager is anything like me, everything is urgent. I am not a difficult person but I get stressed and enthusiastic in equal measure. I can keep throwing tasks and projects at my assistant ad infinitum as I think of them and I trust that as an adult, when it's enough she will tell me.

My previous EA, Matt, who was with me for nine years, often raised an eyebrow and said to me, 'Lucy, of all these urgent things, what is URGENT urgent?'

Timeboxing means that an assistant is able to point the manager to the calendar and ask 'Where?' Not in a disrespectful way, but in so doing you give them the opportunity to decide whether it's really urgent or not.

And if it is, you might shift some things around. And if it's not, it will probably go into the calendar in a couple of weeks' time.

We'll talk more about Timeboxing later in the book.

We've talked a lot about communication already, but to me one of the greatest tools when it comes to communication is your daily meeting, or morning prayers as we affectionately call them in our office. Why morning prayers? Well, I was brought up Roman Catholic and at school we met as a community for morning prayers. That meeting was as much about making sure we were all on the same page at the start of each day as it was about the praying, I suspect, and that is what this meeting is all about.

Simply put, it's the most important meeting of my day. Why? Because once we have that meeting, Fran can get on with her job – which is to make me most effective.

But why only 10 minutes a day? That's for two reasons.

Firstly, we have already established that I have the attention span of a gnat. I really don't do detail unless I am dragged kicking and screaming. Or unless I have cleared a chunk of time to do it. The idea of spending an hour once a week talking about administrative detail is my idea of hell. That said, my 10 minutes every morning allows us to cover a multitude of things, and because the meeting is every day, we CAN cover things in just 10 minutes.

Every morning we cover:

1 What's in the calendar for today?
2 Has anything changed since yesterday?
3 Email communications – is there something she wants clarified
   or to bring to my attention?
4 Staff issues – is there anything she thinks I need to know?
5 Status updates on projects.
6 Upcoming travel.
7 Follow-up items.

Of course, not all of these need to be covered every day. It depends on what happened the day before. But when a meeting is every day, you can cover a huge amount in 10 minutes.

The second reason for only having 10 minutes is that nobody else wants 10 minutes of my time. When you have a meeting that is an hour long, you know that inevitably somebody else will come during the week saying that they have something urgent to discuss with your manager. Be honest. How often do you sigh and take yourself off the calendar so they can have your hour? Stop it! You need your 1:1s. But by making them 10 minutes a day, you are less likely to have to give that time to someone else.

It doesn't necessarily have to be a formal meeting. Melba Duncan talks about how when she was EA to Pete Peterson, former Chairman and CEO of Lehman Brothers, she knew he hated the idea of regular meetings with her.

She noticed that every day, he walked past her desk at about 10 am and came back 15 minutes later. I suspect he went to smoke, but she is too dignified to say so. So instead of insisting on a meeting, she started making a list of things she needed clarification on, in order of priority. And when he walked past her desk she got up and walked with him. She says that one day a few months later, he walked past her desk and she didn't stand up because she was preoccupied and he commented, 'Aren't we walking today, Melba?' They had established their own rhythm.

Similarly, Libby Moore, former EA to Oprah, said it was almost impossible to find time to do 1:1s. But she needed the information. Libby noticed that Oprah had her hair and makeup done on Tuesday, Wednesday and Thursday mornings and again in the afternoon. Just like Melba, she collated a list of questions in priority order and then she sat next to Oprah as she fixed her hair and makeup, asking the questions she needed answered.

Whether they know it or not, this time for answering questions is essential for building understanding, rapport and collaboration with your manager.

I hosted a conference for a secret sorority of top-level assistants in New York a few years ago. One of the sessions was with a panel of CEOs from major companies. The organizers told me I could ask them whatever I liked. So, of course, I took to social media to see what questions you would like me to ask.

The top one by a mile was 'How do I stop them from cancelling my 1:1 meeting?'

So I asked them.

And they blinked a bit. And then they said, 'But don't they manage the calendar?'

And I had a lightbulb moment!

When my staff want to see me, they turn up, one after another, and we talk through what they need to discuss.

When Fran arrives, I don't think, 'What's she doing here?' She is as important a meeting as everyone else. In fact, I would say my meetings with her are some of the most important meetings of the week.

She needs to know the priorities so she can get on with her job. Which is to maximize my effectiveness!

Don't take yourself off the calendar! Your manager needs that time with you – whether they know it or not – to help you to help them.

A final word on 1:1 meetings. If you think back to what I said about communication being 55 per cent body language, 38 per cent tone, pace and pitch of voice, and only 7 per cent words, you will begin to understand the importance of communicating face-to-face. If you are only communicating via email or message, it can take on a tone. Ideally you want to meet either in person or via Teams or Zoom. And if that isn't possible, the next best option is to talk on the phone so they can hear your tone. Email and messaging are a last resort and should never replace your 1:1 meetings.

We've talked a bit about how to work out what your priorities are already, and why, when you're feeling unsure about what to do first, you should ask your executive to clarify priorities.

Especially if you are managing multiple managers, they may not realize how much you've got to do that's not for them and how urgent it is.

FIGURE 6.2   Jug, stones and sand time management analogy

A good way to look at how to manage your time is to divide your tasks into stones and sand.

Imagine that the jug in this picture is your day. Which would you put in first? The stones or the sand? Well of course it's the stones. You can then sprinkle the sand into the glass, and it will fill the gaps. If you try to put sand in first, the stones won't fit.

So what are your stones and what is your sand as an assistant?

The stones are the things you absolutely have to get done today. They are your priorities, things like the board report, or event management, or expenses, or writing a briefing document. Your personal development is also a stone by the way. It should also be diarized.

The sand is everything else: emails you are copied into, people who want to know where the envelopes are, people who come and stand next to your desk to talk to you because they are waiting to go into see your manager but they are 10 minutes early – that stuff!

If we are not careful, we end up just doing sand because it's the small, easily done tasks that give instant gratification and release the endorphins regularly as we tick them off our list. Beware of neglecting the stones – they are what build your career.

A word about those people who you don't report to directly. When they come and ask you to do something for them, please try to remember that this is not what you are employed to do. You are employed to maximize the ROI on your manager's salary. Of course, I am not suggesting for one moment that you should be unhelpful and say no if you have spare capacity, but for most assistants, when I ask them to raise their hands if they don't have enough work, they start laughing hysterically.

I know why you say yes. You are the problem solvers and not the problem creators. But the next time someone asks you to do something for them in a wheedling voice and your brain is saying 'No, no, no', don't open your mouth and say 'Yes' because by doing so you are taking yourself away from your core job.

Instead, get organized. Put together that shared calendar between you and all your executives. Put your stones into the calendar first and then if anyone wants sand – especially if you don't report to them – they come second.

Let's talk a little more about prioritization.

Mark Twain famously said, 'If it's your job to eat a frog, it's best to do it first thing in the morning. And if it's your job to eat two frogs, it's best to eat the biggest one first.'

In other words, if there is something you hate doing – minutes for example I know tend to make most of you shudder when I mention them – then get it done first thing in the morning and then your day can only get better. And if you have two frogs, do the worst one first and then get the second one off your plate. It's a recipe for sanity.

I once asked Matt the questions that he thought were the most important when it came to establishing how to deal with things I was asking him to do. He said:

- find out *why* it's important
- find out what the expectation regarding the end result is
- find out when it's due
- find out what updates are expected and how often

This whole exchange is probably a couple of minutes long. But by asking the questions, he had absolute clarity on expectations. The WHY is one of the most important questions you can ask if you want to become a strategic assistant. Most assistants understand the HOW to get something done, the WHO can help them to do it and the WHAT needs to be done, but the WHY piece is missing. Asking why will give you a totally different perspective.

The key to stepping into effective partnership is moving from being a reactive, transactional, task-based assistant to a proactive, strategic leader.

Can you imagine if Fran and Matt waited for me to tell them what to do? I wouldn't have a business. They made it their mission to understand me, to understand the business and the direction I wanted to take it in, alongside understanding my goals and aspirations so they were able to support at the highest level. This also meant that they had authority and influence in their own right.

As a CEO, I want an assistant who reflects my characteristics but with different skill sets. I am not looking for 'support' that isn't as actively involved in the success of the business as I am. What I want is someone who understands the direction of the business, who is as good a communicator as I am, who is strong enough to lead up and tell me when I am getting it wrong, and who is emotionally intelligent in the way they deal with the other staff.

If you're not being offered the opportunity to become this assistant and you want to make the move, I would think seriously about what it is that you want to do differently. Make a list. And then choose three things to suggest to your executive.

Why only three? Because if you choose more than three you will confuse your executive and you will confuse yourself.

We've talked already about trust but this is a great way to start to build it. When you choose three things that you think will add value to the business if you implement them and take the initiative to suggest and deliver them, and then you deliver them immaculately, the next time you go to your manager suggesting improved ways of doing things, they are far more likely to say yes. This is how you build not only your role but trust over a period of time.

I recently spoke at an event in Seattle. Part of the agenda was an interview about partnership with a CEO and his EA. In it, he expressed his frustration with hiring assistants who were employed to do a role but then didn't want to do that role at all and tried to turn it into something else. I challenged him, asking, 'But surely, if they were doing the work they were employed to do immaculately and they had more capacity and wanted to add value and take on more responsibility, you wouldn't have a problem with that?'

He gracefully agreed with me. It's something to be aware of. No manager will have a problem with you doing something when they can see the value it brings to them as an individual or to the business.

That is key to growing your role. You don't want to talk about what any of this is going to do for you. However much they love you, 9 times out of 10 they don't care. What they want to know is what it will do for them or for the business. So, think about how you are going to measure the impact of what you're suggesting – either in terms of cost savings or efficiencies.

How you communicate your ideas is important too. Going back to our personality types, if they are red, you will want to get to the point quickly. List the things you want to change as bullet points and tell them you want to discuss in more detail.

If they are yellow, you've got some amazing ideas that will make a huge impact really quickly. Paint pictures, use lots of modulation in your voice and get excited.

If they are green, you have three ideas but you want to give them time to think about it. You are happy to try them one at a time and take it slowly so you can see the impact before you move on to the next one.

If they are blue, lead with data. Explain what the impact will be to the bottom line in terms of cost and efficiency savings.

It may be that they have different ideas as to how you are going to progress, or they are only willing to let you run with one of your ideas. This is OK. It's a start, and it still gives you an opportunity to prove yourself and build that trust.

You can always come back to your ideas later once that trust is built.

Before we leave the subject of partnership, I want to introduce one more concept: learning styles.

Our brains are split into two and the left side is all about logic, maths, things that are linear, rational and ordered. The right side of the brain, however, is all about art, creativity, emotion and imagination. Some of us are left-brain dominant and some right-brain dominant. It's interesting in a classroom environment to test this. I ask my delegates to describe the room they are sitting in. The left-brained people say that the room is rectangular and brown. It's all very factual. Whereas the right-brained people say it's inspiring and light and exciting. It's about how it makes them feel. They are both correct. It's just they look at things in a very different way.

Of course, to get information into your manager as quickly as possible it helps to understand which of the two they are. If they are left-brained you should be leading with explanation, discussion, debate and reasoning. Whereas if they are right-brained you should be leading with stories, metaphors, analogies and illustrations.

It's another example of how you can give your executive back time by giving them information in the way that they will absorb it most quickly.

Let's take this one step further though and look at the VAK model. VAK stands for Visual, Auditory and Kinesthetic – the three ways people learn best. When you know your manager's learning style it's going to help them to be more productive, improve the way they solve problems, and help them to make better decisions and be more creative.

Let's take each of them in turn.

Visual learners will learn through seeing and reading. They prefer to use visual information for planning, remembering and decision making. They are much better at remembering faces than names and they prefer to see your facial reactions so face-to-face, Zoom or Teams are probably their go-to rather than speaking on the phone. They prefer written directions and work best with graphs, diagrams and mind maps.

If they are an auditory learner, they are going to learn through listening and talking so it's much better to organize meetings for them so they can talk things through. They'll pay far more attention to the tone of a conversation than the words. They often don't notice what's going on around them visually and remember what they hear rather than what they see. An auditory person would much rather call someone on the phone than meet them face-to-face.

And finally let's look at kinesthetic learners or people who learn through doing. Quite often they have problems with traditional education methods and they much prefer to take part in hands-on activities. My husband is kinesthetic. He started out working as a chef, before becoming an antiques restorer and then a builder. Now retired, he's growing bonsai trees. Go figure! Kinesthetic people are going to make decisions based on how they feel. If you have a manager who looks at all the facts and then decides to go on 'gut instinct' they are probably kinesthetic. It's also worth noting that they tend to speak more slowly than other people. This is because feelings take longer to process than pictures or sounds.

This is the final piece of the partnership puzzle. Let me give you a really good example. Imagine that I need to make a decision based on some figures. It's no good giving me a spreadsheet if I am visual. I need it in a graphic format to make decisions quickly. Or if I'm auditory, maybe you want to arrange a meeting for me to discuss the figures with other impacted managers. But if I'm kinesthetic, you probably want to get me in front of someone from finance so we can work through the figures together.

Can you see how by treating them all differently, you are able to treat them the same? Understanding all these models will give you the insights you need to partner at the highest level.

Reference

Tuckman, B W (1965) Developmental sequence in small groups, *Psychological Bulletin*, 63 (6), pp 384–99

CHAPTER SEVEN

So, you think you're strategic?

So far in the book we have covered all sorts of things that contribute towards you stepping up to become a strategic business partner: understanding how the role has changed, communication and collaboration, emotional intelligence, understanding different personalities and self-awareness. And we've begun to look at what strategic partnership looks like. But now we're going to shift up a gear.

Much has been made in recent times of the emergence of the assistant as a strategic business partner. The term is THE buzzword in the industry. But how do you become strategic? What does it mean? How do you change your day-to-day role to become the assistant that your executive needs to deliver at the highest levels? This chapter is in two sections. The first is understanding the business and the second is strategically managing your executive.

Understanding the business

Knowing is not understanding. There is a great deal of difference between knowing and understanding. You can know a lot about something but not really understand it. Most assistants know a lot about their organization and how it works but don't really understand it.

When you're in a classroom environment, at this point you tend to look slightly offended and argue that you DO understand. So think about your organization in detail. Here's where you suddenly realize that whilst you can answer surface-level questions about your organization, there is still a lot to learn. There is nothing wrong with that. Traditionally, you haven't had to understand what your organization does at this high a level. But as the role transitions into a more proactive, strategic one, your depth of knowledge needs to increase. My purpose by the way is purely to show you where the gaps in your knowledge are, so you can go and find out the answers.

Here are some things you might want to research in order to understand your organization better.

Direction

Do you understand where the organization is trying to get to in the short and long term? We know priorities are changing so fast currently that it's hard to keep up, but there will be a plan. Have you read it? Even if it's just the headlines. When you get called into that quarterly meeting to hear the results of the last quarter and to talk about future plans, if you are anything like I was, you will be thinking, 'Kill me now! I have so much to do, and this is two hours of my life that I am never going to get back.' And you sit there composing emails in your head that need to be sent later. But now is no time to not be paying attention. Understanding where the business is heading and what your department and in particular your manager is expected to contribute to that, and how you can support to actively contribute your skill set to the end result, is a must. What are the goals? It will give you huge insight into how you can step up and where you need to go and learn more.

Geography

What geographical markets does your organization compete in? What kinds of activities are involved in each market? Do you understand which products are most successful in which regions? And do you understand the nuances of the different cultures? Usually, if you keep track of what is working elsewhere, you can see what's coming down the track for you. The hospitality industry for example, always looks to Singapore to see what the new 'next big thing' will be.

If your manager is working across cultures, understanding those cultures is key to supporting your manager and to doing business internationally. Whatever sector you are operating in, understanding culture differences will have a huge impact.

If I am heading to a new country or region, Fran will always prepare me a one-pager on what to expect and whether there is anything I need to know in terms of behaviour, language or customs. I usually even have a few words in the language of the country that I am visiting. I will always try at least to say 'Good morning, how wonderful it is to be here' in the host's language.

Briefing documents also come into play here. I know of one assistant whose manager was heading to Israel for meetings for the first time. There was a big deal on the line and so she decided to write him a one-pager on the history and political landscape of Israel so that he could sound informed and confident. He said being properly briefed changed everything.

SWOT

A common form of competitive analysis in business is to do what's called a SWOT. In it, the team brainstorms either the organization's or a product's strengths, weaknesses, opportunities and threats. You can find free SWOT analysis templates online.

To do a SWOT effectively you need to understand who your competition is and which areas they are particularly strong in, or not. Do you know where your business performs better than the competition? Do you know who your competition is? If I asked you to do a SWOT analysis on your product or area of your organization, would you be able to do it?

Competition doesn't necessarily mean organizations that are competing directly against you now. It can also mean organizations that have the potential to step into your space. If you're not sure what I'm talking about, think Blockbuster video, put out of business by Netflix. Or what about Kodak, put out of business by the mobile phone companies.

If you work for a small business, it could be that tracking what the competition are doing will fall to you. Certainly, Fran keeps an eye on what's going on for me.

There are two great ways to do this and the first is Google Alerts. If you head to your web browser and type in Google Alerts, you will find a box like the one below.

FIGURE 7.1   Google Alerts

Simply add the keywords you want it to search for and set up how often you want to be alerted. Google will then scan the internet for whatever terms you want it to look for on a daily basis. If it finds nothing, you will receive nothing; however, if the keywords appear anywhere on the web, it will send you a notification. You can choose how often it happens – every day or once a week.

We have it set up for my name. It's not vanity. Because I run a global business and am often quoted as an authority on the administrative profession, I want to know what they are saying and what they have quoted me as saying.

I also have it set up for each of our products, for trainers and organizations that we work with, for trainers and organizations that we don't work with but would like to, and of course for our competition. It means we can keep our finger absolutely on the pulse of what's going on across the profession.

So, what does this mean for you? Well imagine for example that your organization is worried about one of the competition or that you are going through a merger or acquisition. How on point would it make you look if you could walk into your manager's office and say, 'I know you're watching what XXX are doing at the moment. Did you see the article that mentioned them in the *New York Times* this morning?' It's such a clever way to keep on top of what you need to know.

The other way to keep track is social media.

There is a great deal of bunk written about social media. In essence it's just networking but online. If you went to an in-person event, you would listen to the conversation and when you thought you had something useful to add, you would say something. Social media is no different.

It is not about broadcasting or selling. We use it primarily for listening. It's a real-time barometer for what's hot currently as well as for gaining insights from our customers. Sometimes I will post about something that I think is really important and there is tumbleweed – nobody responds or likes. Other times it will get thousands of responses. We use the interactions as a way to decide what we should be putting in the magazine. We have turned our customers' conversations into a resource for inspiring innovation.

When I launched my business, I had no money at all for marketing so I learned how to use social media pretty quickly.

We've built a huge community. Our LinkedIn group is just under 50,000 assistants now, all sharing tips, tricks and best practice.

We also use it as a way to energize and build brand stewardship, identifying enthusiastic customers and using them to spread the word to others. In the beginning it was only me posting and occasionally people would respond. Now they are their own community, supporting each other.

So you can use social media and groups like ours as your own community, to ask questions, find resources and sense-check things. But what about also finding groups for your industry so you can track what's going on there? Or following your company so you can see what's being posted, or following stakeholders to get a feel of what is important to them? You can also follow the competition to keep up to date with what they are up to, to ensure you have your finger on the pulse.

Social media used properly is so powerful. It's also worth knowing that according to Glassdoor, 91 per cent of all employers are currently using social media as part of their hiring process.

Social and professional networks were the #1 method employers used to recruit talent in 2021, with 92 per cent of recruiters saying they use social media and professional networks for recruiting (Landes, 2022).

It's certainly worth investing the time in building your profile properly.

Brand values

When we first started the magazine, we spent quite a considerable time brainstorming what our brand would stand for. In the end we came up with 10 words that we wanted people to think of when they thought about us, and even now, over a decade later, when we launch something new, we revisit those words to make sure what we are doing fits with those words.

Could you make a list of 10 words that reflect your organization's brand values – and do you think that if you ran them by the marketing department, they would agree?

And what about your mission statement? Do you know what it is? Usually not, in my experience, unless it's five words or less. Do you know how much money your organization spent on putting that mission statement in place? Tens of thousands of dollars!

And do you know what your customer service guidelines look like? Is there a policy on how your business wants its customers dealt with?

When everyone is clear on these things, the customer journey is so much better. For example, all my staff are clear that we have three hashtags as a business that reflect my brand values.

The first is 'One Profession, One Voice'. It's now been adopted with our permission by the World Administrators Alliance, but I put it in place when I first started travelling the world, campaigning and speaking at events. There were pockets of excellence everywhere that I went, but they weren't working together. We made it our business to start connecting people globally. We went and found every association and network that we could on the planet and there is a huge list of them on our website which is updated regularly. It was one of my career highlights to introduce world-renowned administrator Eth Lloyd and Melba Duncan to each other for the first time in person. Both in their 70s, they had independently been doing almost parallel work to raise the profile of the profession for decades; one in New Zealand and the other in New York. At a stage when they were both starting to think about legacy, it was a privilege to watch them talk about their independent but concurrent journeys. My staff know that to connect people who will be useful to each other is one of our core values.

Or what about 'Changing lives one person at a time'? This started out as the tagline that we came up with for the foundation in South Africa that I am a director of – ISIPHO (it means

'The Gift' in Zulu). We take young people without access to finance for education and train them for a year to become an assistant. And then we help to find them work.

Looking at the number of potential candidates for the bursary was overwhelming but I remember Anel Martin, another director of the foundation, telling me a story. She said that a man was walking down a beach with his young son. The beach was full of starfish washed up on the beach. Every few steps, the son stopped, picked up a starfish and threw it back into the sea. The father said to his son, 'I don't know why you are bothering. There are too many of them. Throwing one or two back won't make any difference.'

'It will make a difference to THAT starfish,' replied the son.

We've lived by that mantra ever since. My staff know that what matters is that one person that we are dealing with in that moment, and they should be made to feel like they are the only person that we have dealt with today.

My third and final hashtag is 'The money is in the conversation' and it ties in with the second one.

People feel respected and you build trust with them when you talk to them, and more importantly actively listen so that they feel valued.

My staff are not in the business of broadcasting to sell a product. We are in the business of building a community. We started a conversation 12 years ago that is still going strong, and I want everyone who joins our community to feel valued and heard.

Can you see how understanding the brand values changes everything? The conversations my staff have and the way we interact would be totally different if they didn't understand what my expectation is.

So how does this relate to you? Well, most of the time, assistants are the first people that your customers will come into contact with. You are a brand ambassador for your organization. How can you be a brand ambassador if you don't understand what the business's brand stands for?

Other departments and the rhythm of the business

It could be that you work for a huge business and that to understand the entire organization at a granular level is neither desirable nor in the best interests of those you serve, but at the very least, you should understand your department and where it fits into the rest of the organization.

When I am training junior assistants, I very often start with a game. I get them to stand in a circle and I hand one of the group a tennis ball. I tell them to throw it to each other so that everyone has a chance to hold the ball and to keep throwing it around the group in repetitive sequence until they have got used to it. When they have, I take the tennis ball away and give a football to someone else in the group and tell them to throw it around the group in a different sequence. When they have got used to that one, I reintroduce the tennis ball. So now there are two things flying around the room in different directions.

Eventually, there are five different things flying around the room. And of course, to start with there is a lot of laughter and balls get dropped but, in the end, they work it out, mainly because they have got their heads around where each object is coming from and where it's going to.

It's a great analogy for business, isn't it? You are given an ever-increasing number of things to do and to start with you drop the ball, but in the end you learn to juggle it all by concentrating hard and learning where things are coming from and where they are going to. A good assistant will understand this as a matter of course and will find a way to make it work. An exceptional assistant will take a step back, will look at everything flying in all directions and will think, this is insanity, there has to be a better process for doing this, and will set about devising one.

Because assistants are so adept at that process and procedure piece, and you have ultimate control over the calendar, you will often find yourself driving the rhythm of either your department or your organization. Don't be scared of that responsibility. It adds huge value to your role to understand how it all fits together.

Stakeholders

What are the values and expectations of those who have power in and around the business? How do they want to be communicated with? Where does your manager sit in the pecking order? Up until now, we have assumed that their relationship with the people that they report to is good, but what if it's not? It's a strange role in that so much of your success is tied up with how successful your manager is. Your job is not to be afraid of them but to be afraid for them. How can you help to manage their reputation? How can you ensure that the flow of the information is delivered in a timely manner? In some cases, you may also find yourself doing the communication work if your manager doesn't get on with their manager or subordinates. And how can you anticipate as much as possible to ensure that you are putting out fires before they happen? Your relationships with your organization's key stakeholders could be the difference between success and failure for your manager.

Business terminology

In the main, assistants know what they want to say, and what you have to share is usually far more valuable than you know; however, you hold yourself back because you don't trust in your ability to use the right language and fear that you will look stupid. Don't do it to yourself. I often think that I should write a book called *How to Speak Business*. It would solve so much.

The very first time I ever attended a board meeting as a publisher, I was about 30 and everyone else in the room was male, white and older than God. They spoke for over two hours in three-letter acronyms, and towards the end of the meeting, I was starting to get slightly hysterical. I think if anyone else had said a three-letter acronym, I would have lost it.

I left that meeting and asked my EA to put together a directory of those acronyms for me, so that for the next meeting that I attended, I would be better prepared. She did a wonderful job of it, so wonderful in fact that I decided to share it with the entire staff list, in case there was the odd abbreviation that they didn't know. The number of people who came back to me and said, 'Thank goodness, I never knew what half that stuff meant'. Better to ask.

Being assertive and confident is a huge part of communication, which is so vital to becoming a strategic assistant. You need to find your voice.

And there's no better way to find it than to attend leadership meetings. I think attending leadership meetings is one of the easiest ways for an assistant to learn about their organization.

Sir Richard Branson's EA, Helen Clarke, attends all his leadership meetings and not to take the minutes. You listen in a different way when you are there in your own right, and anyway there are plenty of apps that will transcribe the meeting for you now so that if you must take minutes, you can complete them after the meeting.

Helen is there to listen to what Richard is agreeing to and then to ensure that he delivers what he's agreed to in a timely fashion. He famously calls her his memory. She also notes what everyone else has agreed to, so she can keep them on track.

And then she watches body language, so if someone hasn't quite got something, he can follow up afterwards to clarify.

But most importantly she has a front-row seat to understanding what's going on in the business. What's coming down the track? Where are there going to be bottlenecks? It helps her to anticipate. And she has learned their language – the language of Richard's business – so she is a respected entity in her own right.

Like everything else, the secret to getting your manager to agree to allow you to attend is to talk about what's in it for them and for the business.

We established earlier in the book that we only remember 20–50 per cent of what we hear. So, you know those conversations when they emerge from one of their leadership meetings and you ask if there's anything that you should know and they give you a couple of pointers – but you know there was so much more that would have been useful to hear! What a shame you weren't there.

So, what's in it for them? I can tell you from experience that being able to be fully present in the meeting rather than having to take notes, because I know Fran will calendar it for me, helps move things along and encourages creativity. She learns so much from those meetings – and I don't have to remember to tell her. She's just there. And she is ever so much more effective day to day because of her increased understanding of the business.

It's going to help you to anticipate workloads, anticipate barriers and take the initiative. It's a total shift in mindset, requiring different skill sets, perspectives and strengths.

I would be looking at it as an excellent opportunity to learn and to be inspired. It's also a great way to grow your network because when you surround yourself with those senior people, they get to see who you are and what you are capable of. It makes problem solving easier too because you now have a much wider and more senior network of people to help, so that you can make a more confident contribution to the business.

Let's talk a bit more about staying one step ahead. How else can you anticipate?

Both Fran and Matt always say that my sent emails are a mine of information. Far more so than my inbox. It gives them a deep understanding of what's going on and I never worry about them having access to them, because it makes their job, and consequently mine, easier.

Or what about reading executive summaries of board reports? Or fixing a regular meeting with the other EAs at your organization – particularly if you are all looking after C-suite executives, to find out what's happening in other parts of the business. And some things will be cyclical – so for example, there are certain events that I speak at every year, so those go into the calendar a year in advance and other things fit around them.

Whilst I'm talking about planning calendars in advance, a tip for you. Time and again people tell me that they have problems taking all of their vacation, because it's never the right time.

My father gave me a great piece of advice when I first started in business over 35 years ago. He told me to plan my vacation so that when I walked into the office at the start of January, it went into the calendar. That way, I would always have time off to look forward to, which in turn helps manage my effectiveness. He had no time for those who were not taking vacation as a badge of honour, arguing that vacation time was calculated to ensure you didn't burn out.

We talked about the glass, the stones and the sand earlier in the book but I want to look at the same topic slightly differently now: the Eisenhower Decision Matrix (Figure 7.2).

Let's look at quadrant one first. This is where most assistants live; in the firefighting and dealing with crisis zone. But when you live in this quadrant, you are entirely reactive, and you don't have time to get involved in the things that will grow your career.

Quadrants three and four are an occupational hazard to be minimized or dismissed entirely. But it's quadrant two that will create the career you want.

Because quadrant two is the strategic stuff. And the only way you will get to it is to Timebox it. At this point in my course, there are often squeals of 'That's all very well but there simply aren't enough hours in the day. I don't have time.'

It's a matter of priorities if we're honest, though. If I were to offer you first-class flights to New York this weekend, a five-star hotel and top tickets to a Broadway show, you would probably make time.

Let's break down quadrant two in more detail. What is it made up of?

FIGURE 7.2   Eisenhower Decision Matrix

It's planning both short and long range, it's making time for proper preparation, it's looking at how to improve your capacity for productivity and it's your personal development.

Then there's devising and implementing systems and processes. We can see things that could do with improving but there just never seems to be time. By the way, there will be some of you who feel certain systems and processes could be improved but you don't do anything about it because you feel it must have been thought through and a decision made to do it that way. As a CEO, I'm here to tell you that this is often not the case. It's simply done that way because it's always been done that way.

It's a bit like that old wives' tale about the child who is standing watching his mother cook fish and asks her why she always cuts the head and the tail off before she prepares it. She answers that it's what her mother always did and goes to ask her mother why she always cut the head and tail off before she cooked it. Her mother also has no idea. She says her mother always did it.

And she goes to ask her mother why she always cut the head and the tail off before she prepared fish – and her mother answers that it was because the pan was too small and fish wouldn't have fitted in the pan otherwise.

Sometimes you know better. Nobody else understands process and procedure like you do.

Strategically managing your executive

We talked about Timeboxing in an earlier chapter when we explored how to create visibility of what you are doing but I want to mention it again here, this time in relation to managing your manager's time strategically.

Timeboxing has been a total game-changer for me. We began using it during Covid-19 when work-life balance became almost impossible. Everything goes into it, not just my work but also things like my 35-minute walk to work and back again and date night with my husband.

But here's where it gets interesting. Firstly, Fran added lunch. It was a revelation. I had spent a lifetime getting to about 3 pm and feeling lightheaded, and then thinking I might as well wait until dinner, or I would eat something unhealthy just to give me a burst of energy. Now lunch pops up in my calendar and I go to buy lunch. It sounds stupid but it's the prompt I needed.

We talked earlier about taking the to-do list and calendaring the priorities to make sure they were done in a timely fashion, but Fran took this one step further.

First, on the days where I have meetings I now have 20 minutes between each meeting. Particularly during the pandemic when all my meetings were virtual, I had got into the habit of doing back-to-back meetings all day because we were in survival mode. But here's the problem with that.

Firstly, it's exhausting. There has been research done by Microsoft which shows the difference it makes to your brain when you take breaks between meetings. When you do back-to-back meetings all day, your brain literally looks like it's about to explode.

Secondly, it's no good for your creativity. I would do one meeting, make copious notes and have lots of ideas swilling around. But when I went straight into another meeting, my brain had to shift gear immediately into a new scenario. And by the time that meeting was over, all my non-formed ideas had gone. A whole day of meetings like that looks good on paper but actually they are not productive or the best use of time.

Not only that, but there was no time to do the work that I had agreed to do. My life was one continuous meeting. And so, I did the actual work that I had agreed to do in the evenings and at weekends. People were constantly chasing me for work that I had promised to do. Talk about a recipe for burnout. Something had to give.

The 20 minutes between each meeting means I do a meeting and then I have time to type up the notes into our CRM and set both myself and my staff tasks to do as follow-up. It gives me time to solidify the ideas that I had in the meeting and get them down. I do fewer meetings but the ones that I do are far more productive.

And I now do no meetings on Mondays or Fridays. Monday is my day to do the work that I have committed to do in those meetings. So now deliver what I have promised on time. If I have a particularly heavy workload, it might spill into Friday, but my Fridays are set aside to work on my business; on new products, on projects and on new revenue streams.

How much better is it for the business to strategically manage my time in this way?

Let's go back to staying one step ahead. What questions can you ask to get the information you need?

I would be focusing on the open-ended questions – in other words, the ones they can't answer yes or no to. How, what, where, when, who, where and why are all your friends. They're going to get you the depth of information you want and give you the tools to do your job properly – the why is particularly important if you are looking at becoming more strategic. Don't be scared to ask questions. The best assistants are endlessly curious. They want to understand everything that's going on, and not just at a surface level. We'll talk more about this when we come on to our chapter on project management.

The only time that you should be asking closed questions, in other words, the questions to which they answer yes or no, is when you want to make sure you have something right.

'So, if I understand you correctly, what you are saying is ABC? Correct?'

As your manager sees your knowledge growing, along with your confidence, the trust will grow, and this is a core element of becoming a strategic business partner.

A word about trust. As Melba Duncan says in her 2011 article 'The case for executive assistants' in *Harvard Business Review*:

> Two critical factors determine how well a manager utilizes an assistant. The first is the executive's willingness to delegate pieces of his or her workload to the assistant. The second is the assistant's willingness to stretch beyond his or her comfort zone to assume new responsibilities.

In other words, you could be the most miraculous assistant in the world, but if there is no trust, it's never going to work. Your manager has to be willing to delegate and not only understand what it is that you are capable of, but trust you enough to do it.

As I said when we talked about Tuckman, this takes time. Don't be impatient. If you've worked for them for less than 18 months, you're still working on the relationship.

Trust is at the heart of all communication and until you have it, you are never going to be able to fulfil your potential. So always do what you say you are going to do, in the timeframe in which you said you were going to do it. And if you suddenly find you can't, let them know before it becomes a problem.

We remember the managers that had a significant impact on our careers and our performance. Think for a moment about the best manager that you ever had. What was it about them that made them so? Good managers typically have your interests at heart; they want to develop you and are comfortable with you being a star and presenting and getting credit for good work.

The best manager I ever had was a very senior publisher called Jim Hay, who took me under his wing. He was always honest with me. He encouraged me to become the publisher he knew I could be but told me off when I wasn't doing what I should be in such a way that I never wanted to disappoint him again. What a great example he was.

He led from the front and never expected anyone to do work he wasn't prepared to do himself. Publishing is a rat race, but he showed me that you didn't have to be a rat to work in it. Or anywhere else for that matter. I left that job with a belief that to be an inspirational leader, you need to set an example and behave properly. It's one of my core values. You can never be truly successful in a role if it means losing your integrity.

I am sure your experiences will be similar, but here are some things that all strong managers have in common:

- they lead by example
- they have integrity
- they set clear goals
- you understand their vision
- they inspire you
- they give you stimulating work that takes you out of your comfort zone
- they encourage your development personally and professionally
- they communicate clearly
- they admit when they are wrong

- they thank you for excellent work
- they expect the best from you
- they assume positive intent
- they understand the downsides
- they give you recognition when you perform

Shall we go to the dark side?

Think about the worst manager that you ever had. What was it that made them so intolerable?

When I talk to assistants, it usually boils down to communication, a lack of understanding of the role, disrespect or an inflated sense of their own self-importance. Here are the most common things that you tell us drive you crazy:

- lack of detail
- no delegation
- no feedback
- no information in advance
- no alignment meetings (morning prayers)
- no empowerment
- lack of clarity or direction
- insists on managing things that you should be doing
- no growth opportunities
- no recognition for your contribution

If you do each role for two or three years, it is likely you will have at least 15 to 20 executives in your career. So, it's wise to invest time to understand your executive better, and to help them to understand you.

Here are some things that you should be thinking about when you first get a new manager.

When are they most approachable? Is it the morning, lunchtime or early evening? Because that's when you should be doing your morning prayers.

What is their preferred management style? Are they red, yellow, green or blue? It will help you understand how to communicate with them.

What behaviours do they reward? If you understand what behaviours they reward, maybe you can behave that way and get rewarded

What are they trying to accomplish in this role? We already talked about this but what are their goals? What are their KPIs? What does success look like this year? And what are they trying to accomplish?

What are they worried about? The only person in the world other than my husband who really knows what I am worried about is Fran. Why? Because her job is to protect me, to have my back. If she doesn't know what I am worried about, how can she do that?

What is their reputation in the company? What is their relationship like with their executives? Up until now we have assumed your manager is a superstar but suppose their reputation is horrible or there is a communication problem between them and one of their superiors. It could be that you will need to step in and do that communication piece. Or gently tell them that they need to be doing something differently.

Who do they respect? If you understand who they respect and why, it will give you clues for your own behaviours and how you gain respect.

How influential are they? If they are influential, or working on an influential project, can you work so closely with them that it improves your influence?

What is their primary motivation? Is it money, or prestige, or security, or family or keeping up with other people? If you understand their primary motivation, you're going to know what buttons you need to press to get things done.

I would also Google them and take a look at their social media. It will give you an idea of who they are and what they stand for.

Lead this process, don't ask permission. If your new manager is brand new to the company, I would fix a meeting with them before their first day. It establishes your relationship with them before they start to establish relationships with everyone else. Reach out as soon as they accept the job.

Take time to prepare an onboarding portfolio for them that includes the things they will need to know when they start. I know the business will also take them through an official onboarding process but providing your take on things will position you as a valuable resource right from the beginning and the information that you put together will come at it from a different perspective.

It could also be that they are transitioning from another department and know a lot about the business already. In this case, a transition plan with all the things in it you feel would be useful to know about their new department could be helpful.

And here are some questions you should be asking right at the beginning:

- How would you prefer that we communicate? (It's a great moment to introduce the idea of morning prayers. Fran and I also use WhatsApp if the world is burning down. If I get a WhatsApp from her my heart starts pounding!)
- Have you ever had an assistant before? And if yes, what worked and what didn't?
- What are some of the jobs that you currently do that I could do for you instead?
- Use this moment to make clear that you will do calendar/email/travel/expenses/minutes/briefing documents/reports and anything else you want to take on.
- Following on from that, initiate a conversation about how they prefer these things to work. For example, explain the tips from this book on calendar management and that you would like to be the only one with access to their calendar and why. Talk about email triage. Find out their travel preferences so you have them when you are booking. Exchange ideas on how you would both like the processes to work for these. Follow up after the meeting with a document that explains what the agreed processes for these are.

- Are there any projects that you would like me to look at? This introduces the idea that you are open to project work and not just reactive tasks.
- What have you got coming up that I need to know about? If you get into the habit of anticipating early on, it will help them to understand how to use you properly as a proactive assistant.
- I would like to attend leadership meetings in order to understand the business so I can support you properly. Would that be a problem? You have all the reasons earlier in the chapter for arguing your case on how this will help them be more effective.
- Who should I put through immediately if they call, and who should I definitely not put through when they call?
- How can I help you to prioritize your to-do list? Introduce the idea of Timeboxing, the 20-minute breaks, set time for doing work.
- What would you like to see me accomplish in the next month/ six months/year?
- What do I need to know about your leadership style that's going to help us work better together?
- Who do I need to meet with to ensure I get all the information that I need to support you properly?
- What are your short- and long-term objectives?

Of course, it could be that you have been working with your manager forever, but have never asked any of these questions. Use reading this book as a reason to go back and clarify – 'I was reading this great book about how to partner better with your manager and there were some really useful questions in it that I realized I have never asked you. Can we go through some of them?'

I would also take a copy of the Global Skills Matrix and tell them what level you are used to working at, especially if they have never had an assistant before. Talk it through with them so they have a clear idea of what you're capable of and are prepared to take on. Take control right from the beginning so they have confidence that you have 'got them'.

One very high-powered assistant that I know always asks for their wallet in the first meeting so she has copies of all their credit cards, membership cards and frequent flyer details. When I raised an eyebrow, she said, 'Start as you mean to go on, otherwise you're operating with one hand tied behind your back.'

I was once on a radio show and the host asked what, in my opinion, an exceptional assistant looked like.

My mind immediately went back to a time when I was in New York. I had been training all day and not unusually I had stayed too long, chatting to the assistants after the course. The problem was that I was due at the airport to board a flight and I had cut it too fine. It was pouring with rain and I couldn't get a cab. Don't judge me, but I had also lost my travel plan, so I had no idea where I was meant to be.

Now 6 pm in NYC is about 11 pm in the UK. But I had no choice but to call Matt from the cab to explain that I was about to miss my flight. He had all the information to hand and re-organized the flight and ground transport at the other end, and let the client know – all in about 25 minutes. By the time I got to the airport I was all set.

Another example was one year when I was going to speak at APC, one of the biggest conferences in the world for assistants. There were about 50 speakers on the programme. For a business like mine which relies on trainers to write articles, to train clients for us and to take part in conference programmes that we organize, an event like this is a great place to discover new talent.

Matt had given me my travel plan. Of course, all of you would do that I suspect. Then he had given me a folder with all the speakers' photos and biographies in it to read on the plane. I suspect some of you would have done that. But when I got off the plane, my phone started to ping. In fact, it pinged so much that I was curious. On closer inspection, I discovered that he had messaged every speaker, as me, via LinkedIn, to say how much I was looking forward to meeting them and that I hoped I got the opportunity to see them speak.

That's an exceptional assistant, thinking outside of the box and being proactive. He was always one step ahead. In fact, usually, when I asked him if he had done something, he would say it had been done a couple of weeks before. It almost turned into a game.

Being proactive is about a shift in mindset:

- Are you asking how will next year be different or are you thinking what must we do differently?
- Are you a follower or a leader?
- Are you travelling without a map or are you clear on the direction you are taking?
- Are you asking what next or what if?
- Are you feeling overwhelmed or do you have a focused action plan in place?
- And most importantly for collaboration and partnership, are you still thinking in terms of 'them' and 'I' or in terms of 'us' and 'we'?

None of this is comfortable. But if you are comfortable right now, you are probably in the wrong profession. Everything is changing so fast that you are going to be outside of your comfort zone until you have onboarded all the information that you need. But as the saying goes, outside of your comfort zone is where the magic happens.

Before we finish the strategy section, I wanted to take a moment to look at the Chief of Staff role because with the role becoming more prevalent, particularly in the United States, there is huge confusion around what it is and how it fits with the administrative profession.

This is a very senior role. A Chief of Staff (COS) is the equivalent of a senior vice president in most companies. It is not a senior assistant role, although I have seen a few senior assistants move into the lower levels of the title once they have received training in change management and people management.

I have included this explanation of the role here because I am seeing businesses that don't understand what the role is, promoting senior assistants and giving them the Chief of Staff title because they are not sure how else to promote them. Unsurprisingly those assistants get highly defensive when we talk about what the role ACTUALLY is. What I am currently seeing when this happens is someone being promoted from amongst the ranks of the EA population and the rest of the senior EAs questioning why, because they are doing the exact same role.

Assistants need clarity so they can decide whether it's something they aspire to and how to work with a COS so there is a clear delineation between the two roles. The CEO, COS and EA should be a powerful triumvirate, but it rarely is because of the lack of clarity.

So, what are the differences between the roles? And how do they work together?

The CEO, the Chief of Staff and the EA should all have one vision and one mission, but the implementation is split between three roles.

The CEO should be facing outwards into the world. They should be driving new revenue streams and relationships. In my case, for example, I spend most of my life on a plane or on a stage. I am building our business by creating strategic partnerships with other businesses as well as delivering for our client.

The EA should be managing the office of the CEO and their day-to-day life. They make sure their time is best utilized, and they give them back time by handling administrative work which they would otherwise have to do for themselves so that they are as effective and efficient as they can possibly be.

And the Chief of Staff faces inwards. They manage the rhythm of the business; they troubleshoot and identify frustrations. They implement new processes and procedures across the business, and they make sure the CEO is focusing on the right things by becoming a stunt double and taking projects or meetings that they can't get to.

I am about to promote Fran to Chief of Staff and hire a new EA. My reasoning is that, now Covid is over, I am back on the road almost full time. This means that there is nobody to run the office and ensure the business's rhythm continues as it should. In addition, there are all sorts of projects that will improve internal process that I have never been able to get to, and she will now have time to do them. But it's a very different role from what she was doing as my EA.

Usually, the CEO, EA and COS are working together on the same projects from different angles. Let me give you a couple of examples.

Supposing I wanted to look at my travel plan for next year and I asked Fran and my new EA to work on it together.

Fran would do the research part. She would probably go back three years and would look at what speaking engagements were most profitable. She would see if there were events that were cyclical that I had to do, and which ones I had agreed to do for free or less money because it was strategic to do so. She would then put together a research document with her recommendations.

Once we had talked it through and I had signed it off, she would then hand it to Germaine, my new assistant, who would book it all in the most cost-effective way possible, taking into account my travel preferences, whilst making sure that I wasn't zigzagging across the world.

Let's look at another example.

Imagine your business has decided to move offices. It's a major project – right? But who would do what?

Well, the Chief of Staff would probably create the specification based on conversations with the CEO and HR on why the move was needed and what they were trying to achieve. Then they would research what properties were available that fitted that spec before creating a briefing document explaining the viability of each property. Maybe they would do some research into what ambience or types of properties encourage the best productivity. And they would think through who the CEO should meet with to ensure this project works and is delivered on time.

Then they would scope the project and write timelines. They would also track the project to make sure all elements are delivered on time.

Meanwhile, the EA would be fact-finding for the Chief of Staff. They would source and collates quotes from suppliers and book meetings with potential properties.

The EA would format reports or budgets, circulate timelines, organize meetings, prepare and circulates agendas for meetings, and prepare and circulate follow-ups.

Once the project got the go-ahead, much of the project's detail would be organized by the EA.

It's a dream team.

The CEO is managing the company.

The EA is managing the CEO.

Meanwhile, the Chief of Staff manages the CEO's priorities and steps in to fill any gaps.

It's worth noting that the COS is not like a CFO or COO where it's an autonomous role. A COS needs the CEO to exist.

A COS doesn't usually have direct reports. Instead, they are managing the business and ensuring that the CEO's reach is maximized by providing information that will help the CEO make decisions faster and more effectively.

But there are no hard and fast roles. The COS can be different things at different companies, dependent on the needs of the organization.

For example, at Google, Marissa Mayer's COS was tasked with being the 'innovator and forward thinker'. They looked for new technologies or companies to acquire and develop. Whilst at Zappos, the COS is not only the 'right hand' to the CEO, but also leads the culture and community. Meanwhile, at Rolls-Royce, the COS heavily responds to the board and shareholders on behalf of the CEO or with the CEO. Three very different roles, all of which fall under the Chief of Staff banner.

If you would like to learn more about the Chief of Staff role and how it is different, a great place to start is to look at the Global Skills Matrix (Figure 1.1) which lists the Chief of Staff role as a Level 5 Assistant but makes clear that this is only obtainable if an EA does the work; this usually means obtaining a university degree in Business Management or an MBA. At the higher levels you would expect a minimum of 10 years of progressive management or an equivalent combination of education and experience. And of course, you will also need experience of strategic planning, performance management, people management, change leadership and succession planning.

References

Duncan, M (2011) The case for executive assistants, *Harvard Business Review*, May

Landes, E (2022) 35 need-to-know social media recruiting statistics in 2022, Careerarc, https://www.careerarc.com/blog/social-media-recruiting-statistics/ (archived at https://perma.cc/MA5B-QNBK)

CHAPTER EIGHT

The productivity piece

At the heart of every assistant's role is the ability to save their managers time and to get things done in a timely fashion because, let's face it, getting more done in less time is a goal for every business.

There are thousands of apps and pieces of technology out there that can improve your productivity, and that's a whole other conversation, but I wanted to look at three of the core parts of most assistant roles: email, calendar and travel management. When we cover this topic on my course, it's a conversation, with the delegates sharing their top tips, and it's always fascinating to me how different people structure their systems.

Let's begin with email. How many emails do you have in your inbox right now? And what does that say about you? Are you one of those people that can't leave the office if there is an unread email in your inbox or do you have thousands of them sitting there that you search when you need something?

Did you know that more than 306 billion emails are sent and received each day (Statista, 2021)? And the average number of emails in an inbox is 200 (Plummer, 2019)?

Are you firefighting and just responding to urgent questions and the people who shout the loudest, or do you have systems and processes set up to manage your email in a structured way?

What is for sure is that we will always have more emails than we would like. We can't control how people communicate with us, but how we send emails and what we do with the replies will help to make them more manageable.

So what are the things that drive you crazy about email? Here are the top 10 from the assistants I have taught in the last year:

1 **Reply all**

   Always top of the list! As an assistant you are probably dealing with not just your own inbox but with a least one manager's inbox too, so when someone sends an email to everyone and the entire business decides to make it a networking event, with everyone chipping in, it's not only painful, but also a huge waste of time. Did you know you can take yourself out of these conversations in Gmail and Outlook? For Gmail, you need to use the 'Mute' button which is housed under the three-dot ellipsis or 'more' menu. For Outlook, simply open a message, go to the delete button and click on the arrow next to it, which will give you the option to ignore. Job done!

2 **Emails that SHOUT**

   All CAPS is the email equivalent of shouting; nobody wants to be shouted at, particularly in a business environment.

3 **No proper subject line**

   We use subject lines in emails to find the information we need quickly and efficiently, so when someone writes to us with the subject line, 'Hello' for example, it sets our teeth on edge. In a world where we are being bombarded with email messages and we are competing for people's attention, a clear, concise subject line is a gift to the recipient. The ideal length for a subject line is six to ten words. Many experts agree that including phrases like 'Please Reply' or 'Response Needed' makes it more likely that an email recipient will respond.

4 **Useless signatures**

A professional email signature should include essential information about you and your business, including your name, job title, company, phone number, address and website link. And ideally, your phone number and address should be hyperlinked so someone can call you with one click or check out where you are based. It's frustrating when you have to copy and paste a phone number or address into your phone to connect. Or even worse, when the signature is a GIF and you can't even copy and paste.

5 **Very long emails**

I encourage my team to make each email one point and no more. Why? Because it is great for my endorphins. Have you ever written something on the end of your to-do list just so you can immediately cross it off again? It's that! When someone sends me a long email with all sorts of things in it that I need to do, my instant reaction is to either shut it, thinking I will come back to it later, or to want to print it so I can tick things off as I do them. It's a source of angst when you manage to tick off everything in that long email except for one thing, because it means you can't get it off your plate and reward yourself with the feeling of achievement.

6 **Keyboard warriors**

If an email has gone back and forth more than twice, pick up the phone or go see them. Emails can take on a tone that you don't intend and people tend to adopt a position on the subject, particularly if the conversation starts to deteriorate. If you don't catch it before this happens, you are just going to make a whole heap more problems for yourself. Cut the passive-aggressive 'as per my last email' nonsense. You want your email tone to be helpful, professional, friendly and concise.

7 **URGENT emails that aren't urgent**
Do you remember the story of the boy who cried wolf? When a wolf finally DID turn up to eat him, nobody believed him. It's a little like that with emails marked urgent. My inbox is full of 'URGENT' or 'TIME-SENSITIVE' email subject lines. It all becomes noise, and sadly you learn who is really urgent and ignore the rest. The problem with this is that it can be missed when something really is URGENT. My advice is to use it sparingly.

8 **Not understanding what the CC is for**
Do you know what CC stands for? If you are old like me, you will remember typewriters and that we made carbon copies of documents by putting a sheet of blue paper between two sheets of paper and pressing pigment onto the second one as we typed. We didn't expect the recipient to do anything when we gave them a carbon copy. It was to be filed or to keep them informed. Similarly, you shouldn't expect a response if you CC someone into an email. Put them in the 'To' field if you want them to do something.
And BCC is even more complicated. It feels dishonest to me. When you BCC an email without the recipient knowing, it is like allowing someone to eavesdrop on your conversation without their knowledge. I would only ever use it if I was sending a group email, for privacy legislation reasons.

9 **Bad spelling and grammar**
As an editor, I am fanatical about this one. A friend very kindly gave me a breadboard as a wedding present that was personalized. The carved part said 'Lucy and Duncans Breadboard'. So thoughtful, but I can't use it. The missing apostrophe sets my teeth on edge to such an extent that it

lives in a drawer. If you know your spelling and grammar is not as good as it should be, use Grammarly or something similar. You are representative of your company's brand, and when you get it wrong, it doesn't just reflect badly on your personal brand but on theirs too.

10 **Lack of structure and clarity**

When I look at an email, I want to be able to see what it's about easily and to be able to navigate it without having to concentrate too hard. So structure the paragraphs properly, add headings, use bullet points and make it simple to read. Life is too short and time too valuable to have to decipher what an email message means or what needs to be done. The main point, conclusion or request is always in the first sentence of my message.

Here are a few other pointers for you.

Don't shoot the messenger, but you should schedule uninterrupted time to process and organize your email, rather than checking it every time you get a new notification. There is an exercise that I do in my training which proves, categorically, that multitasking is a myth.

First, I ask the class to write the alphabet from A to Z, and I time them whilst they do it. It usually takes about 8–12 seconds. Then, I ask them to do the same thing again but with the numbers 1 to 26 and again, I time them. The timing, of course, is roughly the same as for the letters. But then I ask them to hide what they have written, and writing across the page, not trying to find sequences or doing one type first, to write 1A, 2B, 3C etc., all the way through to 26Z. On average it takes them between 48–60 seconds, double what it took when they did them separately.

Why does it work that way? We're back to our friends, the left and the right brain. Letters are the right brain, numbers are the left brain, and we're confusing the heck out of both of them.

Try it! You'll be horrified.

Multitasking doubles the amount of time that it takes you to do anything when you are trying to do two things at once – quite literally. If you want to give yourself back up to 50 per cent of your time, one of the best ways is to focus on one thing at a time. Email is one of the worst culprits for this because every time a notification pops up in the bottom right-hand corner of your screen, it takes your brain away from what it should be doing in that moment. When we turn off the notifications and schedule time to write and respond to email, it makes us far more efficient. A good tip is to run this exercise as a piece of fun with your team to show them how it works. But then explain that from now on when you are writing a report or doing figure work, your out-of-office message will be on and they should contact you by phone if something is urgent. As with everything else, if you position it in terms of what's in it for them – in other words, you will get much more work done in the time given – there won't be any arguments about whether it's valuable or not.

Let's talk about filing, colour coding and how you organize your emails. As a rule of thumb, when you first open your inbox in the morning, whether that is your own inbox or your manager's, it should always be with the intention to triage the emails rather than to deal with them.

It doesn't matter much whether you are filing them or colour-coding them as long as the system works for you and your manager. But it would help if you agreed with all the other administrative professionals at your organization what the system is. I find it astounding that administrative teams don't do this. If, for example, you all agree on the same colour-coding system for email or for calendars, or you all agree to use the same email triage system when someone is on vacation or sick, it makes it so much easier to cover their work because you're not having to figure out how someone else organizes their systems before you do the work.

We use the email triage system that I mentioned in Chapter 1 and I know that thousands of you have adopted it, because you write to tell me so. And your managers love it because they retain control but free up a massive amount of time they would otherwise have spent emailing.

The backstory to this triage system is a good one, and many of you will identify with it because I know how many of you are frustrated with not being able to take over looking after your manager's email. You know how much time you could free up for them and how much more efficient it would make you if you better understood what was happening in their world so you could plan accordingly.

Matt and I were no different. When Matt started working for me, I had over 25,000 unread emails. Matt was always meticulous about his inbox and descended into a gentle state of apoplexy if he had emails in his inbox when he left the office in the evening.

Looking slightly pale, he raised the issue with me and half-jokingly suggested that unless I gave him access, we might need to part company. The decision was not difficult because the trust was there, but we know it's not always that easy to have that conversation.

The trick is to put it in the business terms above and attach the stats. For example:

> Did you know that according to *Harvard Business Review*, the average executive spends 24 per cent of their time dealing with email? I just learned a way that I can take this down to 12 per cent of your time. And the great news is that it's a triage system, so I don't delete anything, which means you can still be in control.
>
> The system is really easy, and it will give you back 12 per cent of your time so you can get on with doing other things. Can I show you how it works, and perhaps we can try it for a couple of weeks to see how it goes?

Believe me, once they have tried it there will be no going back. It has revolutionized my life.

So, back to my story. Once I gave Matt permission to take over, he lifted my entire inbox and put it in a new file which he called 'Beyond Help', and then we went to work to create a new system to triage my email. It works like this.

We have five folders:

1 **Today**

'Today' has everything in it that I absolutely HAVE to answer before I go to sleep tonight. Whether I am on the road touring or in meetings, or in the office, the replies to these emails must be sent today.

2 **Pending**

'Pending' is everything else that needs a response. If I am bored on a long flight or feeling particularly virtuous, I might clear down both folders, but on a daily basis, Fran moves anything that needs doing today up into the 'Today' folder.

3 **FYI**

'FYI' is anything that I need to read but don't need to respond to. It makes for great bedtime or plane journey reading. A lot of these are newsletters and Fran has set rules for them so that they automatically move into the FYI file the minute they hit my inbox, saving her time too.

4 **Fran has dealt with**

'Fran has dealt with' does exactly what it says on the tin. Anything that Fran has already dealt with goes here.

5 **To be deleted**

And finally, 'To be deleted'. To be honest, Fran could probably just delete all of these emails, but I am a bit of a control freak and don't like anything to disappear without me having seen it. This is my safety net. It allows me to go through them and delete them myself, just in case she has missed anything – which is extremely rare. By the way, it's also great for my endorphins to delete all those emails!

Relatively, it takes Fran a lot less time to triage them than it did for me to go through them.

At the time Matt took my emails over, I was getting up to 500 a day and having to work my way through them – and failing miserably. The result was lots of people getting angsty because I wasn't responding in a timely fashion, and me missing out on lots of potential opportunities because I never saw them. The results speak for themselves. I now deal with between 30 and 50 emails per day. I know exactly where I stand. Nothing gets missed, and we are in control.

My inbox stands at just five emails as I write this. It's a great tool to give your executive back their time

And yes, they CAN do it for themselves, but whether they should or not is another question altogether.

One of my top tips for assistants is that the 'holding email' should be your best friend. In other words, you don't necessarily need to know the answer to everything. Replying to an email in your leader's inbox to say that you have seen the email and are having a meeting later this afternoon with your leader and will get an answer for them then, makes you look on top of your work, proactive and efficient.

A couple of other words to the wise. It can get hugely confusing having so many different ways to communicate. Sometimes I open my phone and messages pop up from all directions and disappear again just as quickly. It takes far too much time to go through Facebook Messenger, WhatsApp, emails, Teams, LinkedIn Messages and Instagram Messenger to see if there is anything that I should know there.

Agree on how they want to be communicated with. In our company, all internal communication is now done on Teams. Only external communication is done on email. And if there is an emergency, we communicate on WhatsApp. I will always use the phone or a meeting when I think a communication might be complex, confusing or has the potential to be inflammatory.

And for goodness' sake, particularly if you are stressed when writing an email, write it before you fill in the email address. That way you have the chance to edit it if it's sounding over-emotional.

Moving onto calendar management, I learned another great timesaving tip from international EA trainer Laura Belgrado.

We've been using it for five years, and for me, it changed every-thing. It's around managing meetings.

Firstly, nobody should have access to your leader's calendar except you – other than to view it. If everyone has access to your leader's calendar, how can you be in control of their time in the way that you need to be?

I have lost count of how many times my assistants told me to 'step away from the calendar' in the early days of using this system. It was so tempting just to put in a quick meeting here and there – but then I would ruin everything. My EA has so many pencilled-in meetings on the go at any one time that it screwed everything up for her. The system takes a little getting used to but my goodness it has freed up my brain and my time. It goes like this.

When someone writes asking for a meeting with me, I will always respond saying I would love to meet with them. But I also say that I have copied Fran, my EA, into the email because she will kill me if I start playing with the calendar – and that is true. She controls the calendar with a rod of iron.

Then somewhere under my signature, where nobody looks, I add a discreet code for Fran. It's a number between 1 and 5. If it's a 1 you will get a meeting with me as soon as we can do it. If it's a 5, it will be a cold day in hell before we have a meeting. We also add a further number – 15, 20, 30, 45 – to represent the number of minutes I want to meet for.

Think about the amount of time that frees up over the year. No more talking about how important a meeting is or how long I want it to be. And I don't have to spend time searching to find a time that suits everybody. That is now Fran's job. It's a game-changer.

A well-trained assistant will understand the hierarchy of a business and whose meetings need to be accommodated. They will also understand the ones that take up too much time need-lessly and negotiate how long a leader should spend in those, and they will spot the duds and politely get rid of them.

And if they are initially unsure, they can ask in the morning prayers.

When a leader agrees to cut all access to their calendar and all requests go through the assistant, it revolutionizes managing the leader's time. They become more productive and focused.

It's worth noting that the average leader attends 37 meetings of assorted lengths every week. That's 72 per cent of their total work time in meetings. Did the meeting need to be a meeting at all? Could it have been delegated? Thirty-two per cent of the average CEO's meetings were an hour or more. Did they need all that time? (Porter and Nohria, 2018)

For most assistants, calendar management is a huge part of the job and arguably the most important way in which you can control managers' time and ultimately their productivity. Indeed, some assistants do nothing but play calendar Tetris with their managers' calendars. So it's particularly important that you clarify with your manager how they want you to manage their calendar. How do they want it organized, and what information do they expect to see in it?

A clear and effective calendar will optimize your manager's limited time; without one, whoever shouts loudest will get the attention, and the most important work won't get done.

Consider, what time of day are they most productive? When would they rather do meetings? Do they want you to put time aside for them to do the work? Do they want scheduled breaks? And what about recurring meetings? Are they a good thing or a bad thing? They're a great opportunity to ensure that your manager gets regular face time with their direct reports but you should revisit them regularly. Are they still needed? And is the time set for those meetings appropriate to the time needed or could they be shortened or organized less frequently?

Are you using colour coding for your calendar? It's a great way to see at a glance what your manager is spending their time doing. You should use different colours for different types of meeting and it helps if everyone in your team uses the same colour code so you can deputize for each other easily if needed. Consider conducting a calendar audit for your manager. When you keep track of how they are using their time and write a briefing document with those figures in it, you can have conversations every quarter on whether they are using their time in the way that they want to. You can also take the opportunity to talk through which meetings are no longer necessary or desirable. And what types of activities they would rather do less or more of.

So what should you include in each meeting invite? Fran always includes the following:

- attendees and their contact details
- address (if I am visiting in person)
- agenda, including purpose of the meeting
- supporting documentation
- link to notes on the client in our CRM (if applicable)

And don't forget to set the meeting to the time zone in which it is taking place. That way it will always be correct and you will avoid confusion if your manager is in another country when the Zoom or Teams meeting is taking place.

Outlook also lets you show a side-by-side hourly scale beside the calendar for easy reference. Having Outlook show two time zones at once can be simpler than working out the difference or looking it up each time you're considering the equivalent time at the second location. TimeandDate.com is also an excellent tool for working out perfect meeting times across multiple locations.

Please note that it should only be on the calendar as a meeting if there is an agenda. Supporting documentation to be read before the meeting takes place should also be included in the meeting invite. Nobody should be attending that meeting unprepared and that should be made clear if you are going to maximize your manager's time. The time for reading is not in the meeting itself. The purpose of a meeting is to debate, decide and then discuss. Make sure you have scheduled preparation time for your manager if needed in the calendar. And sometimes they might need a meeting before the main meeting to prepare with another key player. All this needs taking into account.

And after the meeting there should be action points and follow-up items for you to calendar, otherwise it was a waste of both time and money. Do the calculation! How many people took part? How much are they worth an hour collectively? If there are no actions or follow-up items, what was the point? It should have been a phone call or an email.

If your exec is travelling, you may also want to add to the calendar the meeting materials they will need: handouts, PowerPoint slides, etc. and of course their travel itinerary.

Remember that the calendar is a living, breathing document. It's something you should revisit with your manager on a daily basis in your morning prayers so that you can easily reprioritize and regularly re-evaluate whether you are managing it in the most effective way.

And finally let's look at travel planning. What about when they go on business trips?

In my time as CEO of Marcham Publishing, I have been lucky enough to visit over 60 countries so I know a bit about what works and what doesn't. In 2019, I only spent 12 weeks at home.

Here are some things to consider.

We usually have a cyclical events calendar that runs year to year. I speak at many of the same events on an annual basis. These should go into the calendar first. Successful travel planning begins with a skeleton for the year and things get added as we go along, in a sequence that makes sense. Ideally, I don't want to be zigzagging across the world – or as is the case when I am doing my annual three-week tour of the United States, across the country.

Where am I travelling to and who else could I visit whilst I am there? Whenever I travel anywhere, Fran works with my sales team to make sure that my time is maximized to see as many people as possible whilst I am there. Whether I'm flying halfway around the world or visiting a city in my country, it isn't time- or cost-effective to visit just one person. And there is no point travelling to a city for a meeting, only to return a few months later.

All the details for the trip are in the calendar.

Ask them whether they would prefer the fastest, most cost-effective route, or whether they want a layover. For example, whenever I travel to Australia or New Zealand, I will do a couple of days of stopover in Singapore or Hong Kong on the way. It gives me a break in the 27-hour journey and allows me to start to acclimatize to the time difference.

Here are some other key questions that you should ask yourself:

- Is an upgrade possible and if so, what is the process? Some airlines do this for frequent flyers.
- Do they prefer to fly during the day or during the night?
- Are there seat preferences? This can vary by aircraft, but if they have status, you may be able to choose their seat when you are booking, free of charge.
- Do they have special dietary requirements that will mean that you'll need to order a special meal?
- Can you sign them up for programmes that will help them to fast-track? Status will do this anyway; however, TSA or Global Entry in the States, for example, have saved me hours and are well worth the money paid to join the schemes.
- What are their hotel and room preferences? Do they prefer hotel chains with point schemes or independent boutique hotels? Or maybe even an Airbnb? Is a gym a prerequisite? Do they want a pool? What floor do they want to be on – high or low? Do they want a room or a suite? Can they upgrade with their status? Is internet free or paid?
- Do they need vaccinations before they can visit a particular country?

- Do they need a visa? Can they simply order the visa online or do they need to visit the embassy to do that? What is the typical waiting time for the visa to arrive once applied for?
- Is their passport in date? Some countries require that you have six months left on your passport and a certain number of clean pages or they won't let you in.

You may also want to visit your government's advice website. What travel advice are they giving currently, especially if travelling to a less stable region of the world? If this is the case, you may want to include emergency contact details in your travel pack.

And don't forget to check them in to the flight as soon as it is possible to do so, and forward them their boarding pass. Some hotels also allow you to check in online now too.

Of course, you might have a travel agency that handles all of this for you. Many businesses do. But my experience is usually that they lack the personal touch and miss something. It pays to check the detail and make sure it's right.

Let's look at the actual travel itinerary and what you should have on it. It should contain every detail of the trip.

Once this is built, it will go into the calendar with all the other documentation, but you may also want to print a couple of copies. I have lost count of the number of times that I have landed in a new country and the internet has taken a while to connect. My good old-fashioned paper copy has saved my life on more than one occasion. My husband always appreciates having a copy too so he can see exactly where I am and can contact me if he needs to.

Once you have created the itinerary, you can present it to your manager at your morning prayers to see whether there is anything that they would like to add or take out.

Here's a list of things you should be putting in that itinerary, and remember to take account of travel preferences, frequent flyer information and your manager's preferred hotels point schemes:

- Car rental details or taxi pick-up times, from where, going to where, with contact details, timings (pick up and drop off) and how will they be met? At the curb, at the barrier, in the parking lot, in reception?
- Flight number, airline, flight times (take-off and landing), seat number and frequent flyer numbers.
- If your manager has status, where is the location of the lounge?
- How many bags can they check and at what weight?
- Layover/connection times – make sure there is enough time to get from one end of the airport to the other and make sure they are landing and departing from the same airport. In London for example, I usually land in Gatwick and take off again from London Heathrow. That's a one-hour drive from one to the other, and that's before you factor in collecting and rechecking bags.
- Time difference.
- Biographies of people they are meeting, ideally with photographs.
- One-pager with history of the country, culture differences that they should know and a few basic words in the local language.
- Hotel details including check in times, address and contact details. Include some extra details about the hotel's amenities if they are relevant.
- Is there a restaurant onsite? Or where are there restaurants nearby for evenings when there are no meetings?
- Details of company and person they are visiting, including timings, address, contact details and purpose of visit.
- Are they attending any functions with a particular dress code?
- Is your executive meeting the client at a restaurant? Contact details and address should be included.
- Weather – if it's a short enough timeframe to do so. It helps when they are packing.

Sometimes when I am travelling, I can be away for a month. It helps to have the entire schedule from beginning to end in one document, with all these elements. But it also helps to have the day broken down on a daily basis in my calendar.

I would also include copies of their passport, their insurance documents, visas, their Covid certificates and any priority entry schemes they belong to. A copy of these should also be kept in the office in case of emergencies.

As I said at the start of the chapter, your success as an assistant centres around how productive you can make your manager and how much time you can save them. But these tips are also about ensuring that your time is best spent.

References

Plummer, M (2019) How to spend way less time on email every day, *Harvard Business Review*, 22 January

Porter, M and Nohria, N (2018) How CEOs manage time, *Harvard Business Review*, July–August

Statista (2021) Number of sent and received e-mails per day worldwide from 2017 to 2025, https://www.statista.com/statistics/456500/daily-number-of-e-mails-worldwide/ (archived at https://perma.cc/V4BP-KWHW)

Resource

Seeley M (2016) *The Executive Support Guide to Taking Control of your Inbox*, Marcham Publishing, Surrey

Seeley, M and Esquibel, M (2021) *101 Ways to Supercharge Your Productivity*, Marcham Publishing, Surrey

CHAPTER NINE

The future is hybrid

Everything just changed – or did it? For many assistants, just like the rest of the world of work, the way the future of work looks is very different. But at its core, what you are doing on a day-to-day basis remains the same.

In this chapter, I want to look at what hybrid working looks like for you and why it becomes more important than ever that your communication and collaboration skills are where they need to be. The post-pandemic world of work is one of the greatest opportunities you will ever have to step into the role as you have always wanted it to be. This is for several reasons.

Firstly, it has never been more important for executives to be doing the job that they are paid to do. They need to lose the administrative details that they have clung onto for so long so they can deliver the value that their organizations need.

Secondly, the business world seems almost obsessed with measuring the value of every employee as we emerge from the crisis, and for the first time, this includes the assistants. As Peter Drucker said, 'What gets measured gets improved'. The trick for

HR is to understand what to measure, the value of the data they generate and how to make sense of it all to inform decisions.

Here are some of the questions that businesses are asking us for the very first time. I include them because I want you to understand where their thinking is.

1 How do we create a structure for the administrative function which brings order to the relatively chaotic way in which assistants are currently employed, trained and promoted.

2 How do we monitor performance to stop it being based on opinion rather than fact?

3 How do we make sure the executives are using their assistants properly?

4 How do we align skills with needs to make sure that the right assistants are looking after the right executives?

5 How do we ensure we are getting return on investment from our administrative function? And that we have clarity on the value that each assistant is bringing to the business?

6 How do we ensure there are clear goals and KPIs for each admin?

Can you imagine if your organizations answered these questions and acted on them? It would totally change the way the profession is perceived, the way you are managed and how you are utilized. Exciting, isn't it?

And thirdly, I want you to remember your core strengths – process, procedure, communication, collaboration, emotional intelligence, problem solving, people skills, digital skills, self-management and service orientation. All of these will be key for any organization wanting to adopt a hybrid, flexible way of working.

When Covid-19 sent us all home to work, live and play within our four walls, for many of you who had been told for years that flexible working wasn't an option for an assistant because you couldn't do the job properly from home, remote working suddenly became a reality.

Now that the pandemic is over, it's my belief that the future of work is about choice. The press continues to be divided in its opinions on whether working from home is a good thing or not, as are the world's companies. Some are using it as an opportunity to dispose of expensive real estate and are encouraging their employees to work from home. Others are not so happy; they see hybrid working as a threat. It means they lost control. And whilst many have settled into a routine of being in the office for a set number of days a week, and at home for others, it's still working itself out. Being told you have to be in the office on a Tuesday, Wednesday and Thursday is not flexible working. Flexible working is choosing the right way to work for you, whether that is from home or from the office or both.

But can an assistant work successfully from home, or do they need to be in the office? I would argue that absolutely an assistant can work from home. Matt and I did it for nine years. We rarely saw each other. And last year, Fran spent five months living and working in Stuttgart. What difference does it make if I am not in the office myself? But it does need a proactive focus on communication, and an understanding of goals to make it work properly.

I think the question is more about whether the assistant has the resources to do the job properly from home. The CEO of a multinational business recently asked me whether I thought his administrative function could work from home. He was hoping to move in that direction, seeing it as a cost saving. But he was astounded when I suggested that if he was moving in that direction, he would need to do an audit of each assistant first to see whether they had space for a desk, what their Wi-Fi bandwidth was like, whether their chair was ergonomically friendly and what equipment they had.

It hadn't occurred to him that some people wouldn't have a spare room or the financial resources they would need to set themselves up properly to work from home. I have seen enough assistants working from their bedrooms, often sitting on their beds, to know that this is a real issue. I suggested that maybe they would like to subsidize, to ensure either that their employees had the right equipment to do the job or that the organization provided access to a shared workspace.

According to Accenture's The Accenture Future of Work Study 2021, more than two-thirds of workers say they're concerned about returning to the office full time because whilst it may come with benefits like increased productivity, less loneliness and firmer boundaries between work and home life, we have enjoyed not having the commute and the expense that comes with that. We have spent more time with our families and got used to being able to put the laundry on at lunchtime or being there when our kids get home from school.

Not only that, but we worry about how it will work long term. There is still uncertainty and transitions naturally spike our anxiety. You'll feel anxious about returning to something whenever you've stopped doing it. Our routines have changed, as have our social relationships and boundaries. No wonder it all feels so up in the air.

I remember vividly the first time I stood on a stage and talked to real people after Covid. It was at an event in London called The PA Show. It was the first time I had been in a room with so many people in almost two years. I could see their facial reactions and body language instead of looking into a camera and I had to react to those. It was something I hadn't taken into consideration, and it was utterly overwhelming. Afterwards, I returned to my hotel and cried. Really cried. For the people that had been lost, for the fact I had made it through, for finally being able to allow myself to breathe out after two years of holding my breath and with exhaustion from the interaction that I hadn't had in so long. At times over Covid I had wondered whether I would ever stand on a stage again and I will never take visiting other countries for granted again.

We asked assistants about the best and worst parts about working from home or from the office.

The biggest struggles when working from home included not having good enough Wi-Fi, loneliness, juggling work and looking after children, not having dedicated space to work in, not having access to technology, staying motivated, not being able to unplug and taking vacation time.

The things people love about it are not having to commute (with the time and expense this involves), being able to have a more flexible schedule and being able to work from anywhere (my daughter works from home a lot and has been known to travel over a weekend to spend a couple of weeks with me in Spain. We both sit and work during the day and go on holiday in the evening). Other benefits include being able to spend more quality time with children, fewer interruptions, a reduction in office politics and more time to do things because the commute is cancelled, which results in a better work-life balance and a healthier lifestyle because there is time to cook healthier food earlier in the evening, to exercise and to go to bed at a reasonable time.

Sounds idyllic but there are also myriad reasons for wanting to be in the office. Not everyone has children or lives with a partner. That can get horribly lonely. Many like the structure of going into the office. I took on an office when I moved to Spain. It's a 35-minute walk away from my home on purpose so that I have to do my 10,000 steps a day, so that I see something beautiful every day as I walk along the seafront, and so that I have time at the end of every day, after I have closed the office door, to decompress. The exercise has as much to do with maintaining my mental health as it does my physical health.

And then there's technology; it's often faster and more advanced in the office. Or what about meetings? Many people much prefer to have meetings in person than online. And many with children told us how useful it was to have space in which to think and create. It's hard to do detail when there is no quiet space in which to do it. Many felt there was a better routine and rhythm to the day in the office or that it was hard to do the job properly when they couldn't see what was physically going on in and around the business. And finally, many were worried about how visible they were from home. Many people felt that assistants were often invisible in companies before the pandemic. Working from home could make that worse.

Of course, this all depends on whether other people are in the office. The Accenture Future of Work Study 2021 found that 83 per cent of employees would rather work from home and that hybrid workers are more likely to be thriving, while onsite workers are more likely to be disgruntled. It's hard to see what's going on in and around the business if everyone else is working from home. And what's the point in trying to be visible if nobody else is there? We need to reimagine how we communicate and ensure we are still visible when we are working from home.

We are never going to go back to the way we worked before Covid. Work used to be somewhere we went. Now it's something we do. At the time Henry Ford set up his factories and invented 9 to 5, it was an innovative way to attract employees, many of whom were used to working 12-hour days. But it's outdated. It might have worked in Ford's day, when the more hours you worked, the more cars you assembled. But it doesn't work like that in an office where it's far more goal oriented.

The future will be focused on goal setting instead. As long as you hit your goals and complete your work by the set deadline, nobody will care when or for how long you worked on it.

It's ridiculous to think that if you are in the office from 9 to 5 then this is directly related to your output and that somehow if you put in X number of hours, you will make X amount of revenue. It doesn't work like that. This kind of traditional schedule is counterproductive to an employee's ability to tap into their creativity, innovation or teamwork. Productivity will no longer be measured by how many hours we sit at our desk; instead it will be measured by the quality of work produced.

It's why it is so important that you understand your managers' goals and KPIs so that you can work with them on achieving them, and to have your organization set clear goals and expectations for its administrative functions. If this is how performance will be measured, we need to understand exactly what our goals are, what success looks like for us and what the expectations are for our role.

Business growth in an uncertain world depends on the health and happiness of an organization's employees. Companies are realizing that employee productivity and motivation is directly related to how happy they are. We're seeing a shift of focus towards employee happiness, with some companies even going as far as to employ a 'Chief Happiness Officer'.

Part HR and part internal comms, this is not a nonsense position. Making sure employees feel valued and listened to, making sure their salaries and working conditions are good, giving them the freedom to organize and adapt their work schedules to fit around their personal life, supporting their growth, helping them to manage their time better and generally creating a more positive work environment where employees actually enjoy their work are core to the role. The more power employees feel they have when it comes to their contribution to their organization and how it works, the more emotional energy they will invest in it and the more productive they will be.

The stats are mindboggling. Snacknation's Employee Happiness Statistics for 2023 (Bell, 2023) showed that:

- Companies with happy employees outperform the competition by 20 per cent.
- Happy employees are 12 per cent more productive.
- Employees who report being happy at work take 10 times fewer sick days than unhappy employees.
- Fortune's '100 Best Companies to Work For' enjoyed a raise in stock prices of 14 per cent per year from 1998–2005, compared to 6 per cent for the overall market.

What does this have to do with you? I am a great believer that assistants build culture, and in the past few months, I have seen several senior assistants take on the role of Chief Happiness Officer. It's a perfect fit for an assistant's skillset.

One of the first questions I have been encouraging them to think about is 'What is the office for? What is its purpose?' This is at the heart of the debate about returning to the office or not, because if you would rather not be there, your manager is working from home or away on business and you are going to the office to do exactly the same things as you are doing at home, then what's the point? Do you know what senior management's expectations are for when you are in the office or are they just telling everyone that they must be in the office for a certain number of days a week, regardless?

Over the last two years, we've worked out how to do our jobs effectively from home. So how are we going to encourage employees to want to be in the office now that the pandemic is over? What is its function when an office is no longer necessary for productivity?

There needs to be transparency, which means asking lots of questions to ensure clarity in the vision and thought process as to why you need to be there. We need to start thinking about the office as an add-on, as a basis for engagement, collaboration and building company culture.

This could involve reimagining some office space as an informal place to network and socialize. As human beings, we need face-to-face interaction with others and having more communal areas where we can meet informally is a great way to bring the team together.

Or what about utilizing some areas as places where staff can meet for coffee or lunch? Maybe designate some outside space as a picnic area?

You'll need more space for meetings, particularly brainstorming sessions, alongside the technology that makes it possible for those working remotely to join and not feel excluded. And quiet places for those wanting to get away from a more chaotic homelife to ideate effectively.

There may also be areas designated for mentoring, learning and training – something that entry-level staff have been robbed of during the pandemic.

Health and well-being is also a hot topic. Even before Covid we saw moves towards better support with mental health issues, access to nature, on-site exercise and mindfulness programmes, and free healthy food. By providing resources to support more positive lifestyle choices when visiting the office, and by creating spaces that are less structured and more creative, we can reframe the office as more of a destination than an obligation.

The hybrid work environment greatly impacts how you do your job, not least because we have shifted from being a connection-based role to one centred on workflow.

In order to work effectively from anywhere, we need to modify how we communicate because at its heart, this role is still all about communication. The rules we have talked about in the book so far still apply. The role has not changed. It's just that the way we are doing it has shifted.

Workflows are a structured series of steps that take you from the beginning to the end of a process. They make it clear which tasks haven't been started yet, they alert you when someone starts working on that task, and then show what tasks have been completed. We can see at a glance who is responsible for what and how each task is progressing, which increases visibility and efficiency across teams, especially when we are all working remotely. And of course, workflows work perfectly with goals because once you have set goals and an action plan to make them happen, your business can track those actions to ensure you are on target to hit your goals. It's going to be much easier for everyone to see exactly what you are contributing and where you are adding value.

So, what do you need to be successful in the new hybrid world? We've already addressed my top three in previous chapters:

- communication skills
- collaboration skills
- an understanding of goals

But after that, top of my list is a high level of digital skills. Over the pandemic, many senior assistants confided in me that prior to Covid, they had reached a level where they hadn't needed their digital skills to be finely tuned because their roles hadn't demanded it. They had let them slide. They had a rude awakening as digitalization, automation and remote working became the norm and digital skills suddenly became critical to the role. If your digital skills are not where they should be, now is the time to sort that out.

Then, I would be honest with yourself about where you are mentally. Covid triggered a 25 per cent increase in the prevalence of anxiety and depression worldwide according to a scientific brief released by the World Health Organization in March 2022. If you're not 100 per cent, whether you're about to have a full-on breakdown or are classed as what the UK calls 'the worried well', if your mental health is not where it should be, you should be taking steps to get help.

Next is a desire to participate in learning. The World Economic Forum's Future of Jobs Report (2020) says that 50 per cent of workers are in need of reskilling. Make sure you are front and centre when it comes to requesting training. It's going to be vital to keep your skills current and fill any gaps in your knowledge as the future of work evolves.

You should also look at your work-life balance. Is it where it should be? In her book *Time Management for Entrepreneurs and Professionals*, Abigail Barnes talks about the 888 formula, which is a practical framework that helps individuals audit their life against three key metrics and identify where they are unbalanced. It's based on the premise that we all have the same 24 hours, and if we divide those 24 hours into work, rest and activities, we should have eight hours for each. It can be shocking when we figure out our numbers – and life-changing. The first time I heard Abigail present, I realized my numbers were 13 hours of work, seven hours of sleep, and only four hours for activities (everything else). What are your numbers?

All these are your responsibility. But what about what you need from your organization in order to make it work?

Top of my list here is an agile mindset – in other words, everything is changing so fast and we are all still trying to work out what that looks like for us. We have a once-in-a-lifetime opportunity to recreate how we structure our work life to give us a better balance. The Bureau of Labor Statistics 2021 Business Response Survey estimates that 50 million jobs are currently work-at-home capable. There are no definitive reasons for many job functions to require people to come into the office every day.

Organizations need to pay attention to the tide of opinion and stop dictating. I have heard from numerous recruitment companies worldwide that they are having problems recruiting for organizations that are trying to return to full-time office-based work. The Accenture Future of Work Study 2021 tells us 47 per cent of employees would look for another job if their organization didn't offer hybrid working.

Whilst the most striking figure to emerge from the third edition of McKinsey's American Opportunity Survey is that 58 per cent of Americans had the opportunity to work from home at least one day a week, with 35 per cent reporting having the option to work from home five days a week.

Not only that, but the report says that when people have the chance to work flexibly, 87 per cent of them take it. What started as a necessity during the pandemic has become a total shift in the way we work and conduct business.

It's an exciting time. If we ask questions and listen, and learn, we have the opportunity to reestablish the boundaries. What is working in other organizations? What is the research telling us? We need to remain open minded. And think through exactly how it's going to work if we are no longer all going to be in an office together. This is where you come in, by the way, because all of this is going to need new processes and procedures.

For example, have you thought through:

- What system are you going to use for collaboration? The days of working an email-based system are long gone. Internally, we don't use email at all anymore. It's far more effective to use online collaboration tools. Transitioning to remote collaboration can be difficult, but particularly when it comes to managing project work, introducing a system like Microsoft Teams, Slack, Asana, Monday or Trello will be invaluable, particularly when it comes to employee engagement. Everyone is clear on where they have their part to play, on timelines and on goals. You can set clear priorities and objectives so that everyone on your team focuses on what's most important and then track progress and update each other throughout the week. Another huge benefit then is the visibility this will give your stakeholders.
- Where are you going to store information? If you're no longer in an office and are unable to ask each other questions, finding the information you need efficiently and in a format that is easily accessible becomes critical to workflow.
- Knowledge management has never been more important. Knowledge is one of your organization's most valuable assets. Storing, growing and sharing that knowledge is critical to any organization. McKinsey's report, 'The social economy: Unlocking value and productivity through social technologies' indicates that a well-thought-out knowledge management system could reduce information search time by as much as 35 per cent and raise organization-wide productivity by 20 to 25 per cent. Meanwhile, The International Data Corp (IDC), a Framingham, Mass.-based market intelligence and advisory firm in the IT

and telecommunications industries, highlighted that Fortune 500 companies lose roughly $31.5 billion annually by failing to share knowledge (Babcock, 2004). Think about how much knowledge goes with an employee when they leave, or how much time is spent reinventing the wheel. I have long maintained that knowledge management sits very comfortably within an assistant's portfolio. When knowledge is gathered proactively by someone adept at listening and recording process and detail, particularly around what best practices are, what processes need mapping and what ideas are being worked on, the benefits are immeasurable.

- How are you going to communicate? We've already established that communication is critical to the success of the partnership with your manager. For hybrid working to succeed, effective communication must be at the heart of everything you do. If we don't focus on getting this part right, it's potentially a high-risk area. How does your manager want to be communicated with? Which personality type are they? What are their learning styles? When communication is not well managed, it can result in poor information flow, knowledge gaps, barriers to effective teamwork and exclusion of team members who are not in the office. What can you put in place to ensure you, your team and your manager(s) communicate effectively in a hybrid world?

- How does each team member want to work? Do we need everyone to be in the office at the same time? Have we asked each member of staff how they would prefer to work? Do we know their ideal work situation or how many days they would like to be in the office, and which days they are?

- How are we going to run meetings? We want to ensure those working from home feel as involved as those in the office. We decided early on that if one person was online for a meeting, we should all be online to operate from a level playing field. It's also worth considering whether certain team meetings should always be conducted in person.

- Have you agreed on how you want to work as a team? What does normal look like? Have you agreed on response times? How will you ensure teammates who aren't in the office still have a voice? What are the agreements around vacation or sick leave? What are the boundaries?

It's obvious from the above that unless your company's digital technology is where it needs to be, it makes online collaboration hugely difficult. Time and again, I see businesses jumping over dollars to save dimes by not keeping up with the latest technology that would save them money in the long run.

If I'm honest, as a CEO, there is so much going on and so many balls to keep in the air that when my team came to me and suggested that we should start using Teams, they had to drag me kicking and screaming to get me to embrace it. I could see the potential of course, but I was also weighing that up with the time it would take us to move everything over and get used to using a completely different system.

The team put together a business case to explain how it would address the business's needs and what the return on investment would be if we adopted it. They also provided a comprehensive implementation plan.

Like most things, getting your organization to look at adopting new technology is not about what it will do to help you. It's about looking at how it will help your manager and the organization to make cost and time savings.

Here is a great structure for your business case:

- **Identify the pain points**
  What are the problems and how will this technology solve them? For example, you could be working in a remote team and are currently using a spreadsheet which is complicated, time-consuming and leaves room for error. You need a new way to update and share information.

- **Identify the benefits**
  How will the new technology help solve the problem? What are the benefits? Will it save money or time or reduce errors?

- **Use real-life examples**
  Use a real-life example to show how it will benefit your organization. What will it do for your team or department?

- **How does it work?**
  It helps to paint a clear picture of exactly what the new technology is capable of. What are the key features? Can you guide your manager through the process of using it?

- **Estimate the return on investment**
  Presenting your new technology as the solution to all your organization's problems can be tempting. Be careful. You want to under-commit and over-deliver so if it's adopted, everyone sees the new technology as a huge success. So, make calculations based on conservative estimations.

  Want to look at what the return on investment will be? Look at a conservative time saving that will come from implementing the technology. Then work out the average salary across your department and how many people there are working in it (you may need to ask HR for this information). Now multiply the time saved by the average hourly salary and then multiply this by the number of people. This will give you your cost saving.

- **Implementation plan**
  One of the biggest things putting your manager off adopting your new technology will be how to roll it out with minimal disruption, as any disruption equals lost productivity and therefore lost money.

  Put a strong implementation plan in place, and half the job of selling the idea to them will be done. By laying out a clear plan in your business case, you can remove the fear of the unknown and make the decision easier to make.

Aside from being agile and digitally mature, the other thing organizations need to do to ensure success for their administrative professionals in the new world of work is to train them so their skills are honed. If we want to develop the role for the future, we need to reclassify the assistant role as 'talent' instead of as a 'resource'.

When I ask businesses about what training they offer their assistants, nine times out of ten they proudly tell me they offer Word, PowerPoint or Minute Taking. All very nice, but when I ask 'what about leadership or communication or working in partnership or collaboration or business strategy', these things have never occurred to them, although they almost always instantly see the benefit.

In our latest survey, over half the assistants we spoke to said their organization didn't have a training budget in place for them, and 37 per cent said that they had self-funded their personal development in the last year. Only 12 per cent said that their company offered assistant-specific training.

If you look at the questions being asked by organizations at the top of this chapter, the need for assistant-specific training and career progression opportunities becomes obvious. How can an organization expect world-class service from its administrative function when it isn't investing in it?

In her article 'The need for inclusion', Simone White takes this idea one step further, arguing that as administrative professionals, we are often excluded as a profession.

She cites several examples:

- Team events where everyone is invited except the administrative team.
- Team meetings where the team assistant does not attend or, if in attendance, they are seen but not heard.
- Few training and development opportunities, particularly in the case of targeted sessions for administrative professionals.

- Lack of defined career paths or progression structures – progress is often linked to the individual or the team the assistant supports rather than an individual's experience, skillset or impact.

When we dig deeper into our profession, we see how this lack of visibility results in exclusion for administrative professionals even where structures do exist to increase inclusion.

Simone's employer is launching a Learning and Career Development Framework to support their administrative professionals further their careers. This change occurred because a group of administrative professionals understood and articulated their impact on the business.

As Margaret Mead is attributed to have said, 'Never doubt that a small group of committed individuals can change the world – indeed, it is the only thing that ever has.'

Changing the perception starts with us. We all have our part to play, and coming out of Covid, we have the best opportunity we have ever had to step up and transform the role into one that is seen as vital to our organizations, where they clearly see the value and what the ROI is, and where we finally have a seat at the table.

You shall, you will, and you must take the opportunity with both hands. It's no good waiting for someone else to do it. We each are responsible for making a case for why businesses need to retain and elevate their administrative functions. It's not enough to listen and agree. You need to be the change.

References

Accenture (2021) The Future of Work, https://www.accenture.com/content/dam/accenture/final/a-com-migration/pdf/pdf-155/accenture-future-of-work-global-report.pdf (archived at https://perma.cc/ND6P-KYY6)

Babcock, P (2004) Shedding light on knowledge management, https://www.shrm.org/hr-today/news/hr-magazine/pages/0504covstory.aspx (archived at https://perma.cc/92LB-Q6TR)

Barnes, A (2020) *Time Management for Entrepreneurs: How to turn time into profit*, Neilson

Bell, A (2023) 11 shocking employee happiness statistics that will blow your mind, Snacknation, https://snacknation.com/blog/employee-happiness/ (archived at https://perma.cc/HA3M-CUSF)

Bureau of Labor Statistics (2021) Business Response Survey, https://www.bls.gov/brs/2021-results.htm (archived at https://perma.cc/WXZ4-UYHV)

McKinsey (nd) American Opportunity Survey, https://www.mckinsey.com/industries/real-estate/our-insights/americans-are-embracing-flexible-work-and-they-want-more-of-it (archived at https://perma.cc/5E2V-4Y2L)

McKinsey (2012) The social economy: Unlocking value and productivity through social technologies, https://www.mckinsey.com/industries/technology-media-and-telecommunications/our-insights/the-social-economy (archived at https://perma.cc/3478-C3U7)

White, S (2022) The need for inclusion, *Executive Support Magazine*, https://executivesupportmagazine.com/the-need-for-inclusion/ (archived at https://perma.cc/U5RY-KSRQ)

World Economic Forum (2020) The Future of Jobs Report, https://www.weforum.org/reports/the-future-of-jobs-report-2020/ (archived at https://perma.cc/NY7E-547J)

World Health Organization (2022) COVID-19 pandemic triggers 25% increase in prevalence of anxiety and depression worldwide, https://www.who.int/news/item/02-03-2022-covid-19-pandemic-triggers-25-increase-in-prevalence-of-anxiety-and-depression-worldwide (archived at https://perma.cc/2ZSF-65CX)

CHAPTER TEN

Project management

Project management seems to be overtaking the executive assistant's world these days. Whether or not your company calls it 'project management' and deliberately applies its terminology and principles doesn't matter; the reality is that project management is now part of every assistant's working life.

There is a good reason for that. Your skill sets are exactly what a project manager needs because it combines detailed technical skills and processes like budgeting, scheduling and documenting with people skills like leadership, motivating, listening and empathizing. There aren't many other people in your business who excel at both and both are equally important to the process.

By the way, if you find yourself doing more project work than anything else, go get a qualification. In the main, project managers are paid a darn sight more than administrative professionals. The same is true if you are spending most of your life focusing on data analysis.

I am going to use the framework of putting on an event as the template for this chapter on project management because our research shows that it is something that 87 per cent of assistants do, so you already understand how to do it. You just need to be shown how to manage it as a project. You will be able to apply this framework and approach not only to successfully put on events, but also to lead projects of any kind.

It also helps that I have over 35 years' experience in organizing events. In my time, I have worked on everything from small meetings to an event across 12 London boroughs for over 30,000 people so you get the added bonus of gaining some tips and tricks in this chapter for organizing events.

Let's begin by looking at what a project is and what separates it from the rest of your work. All projects:

- will have a beginning and end date
- will have a clearly defined goal
- can involve a single organizational unit, or multiple
- will have a defined resource allocation in terms of time, money or people
- can be a full- or a part-time activity
- will produce a tangible output
- will involve carrying out a non-repetitive task

Having said that, I regard the conferences that we put on all over the world as individual projects in their own right. Although it could be said that the process is repetitive, each event is held in a different country, in a different venue, with different speakers. It helps workflow to manage each one as a separate project.

The official definition of project management from the Association of Project Management's APM Body of Knowledge 7th edition (2019) is the application of processes, methods, skills, knowledge and experience to achieve specific project objectives according to the project acceptance criteria within agreed parameters. Project management has final deliverables that are constrained to a finite timescale and budget. Sounds horribly dry, doesn't it? But managing a project is not dry. For many assistants it will be one of the few times that you get to manage something from beginning to end. It's creative, challenging, thought-provoking and you'll get to show what you're made of. It will also often give you the opportunity to manage people who work at a higher level than you.

I think a lot of bunk is written about project management; much of it is smoke and mirrors. They overcomplicate it to perpetuate the myth that only someone who has been trained and certified can do it properly. But when you take away all that mythology and business speak, what remains is actually a pretty easy process.

FIGURE 10.1 Lifecycle of a project

Lifecycle of an event

1. UNDERSTAND THE EVENT

2. PLAN THE EVENT

3. IMPLEMENT THE EVENT PLAN

4. COMPLETE THE EVENT

If you look at the graphic and you already organize events, you will recognize that you are really good at quadrants 2 and 3. You know exactly how to plan an event and how to implement that plan. But quadrants 1 and 4, not so much. And that's not good because both these stages are really important.

When I teach project management as a class, at the end of the session, I give everyone a two-hour exercise to do, which involves taking a scenario and project managing an event around that scenario. Even when I say very pointedly to my delegates to make sure not to miss out stages 1 and 4 because it's the difference between being an assistant that organizes events and being a project manager, they still go straight to the planning part. This is even when I have told them that this is exactly what they are going to do, that I am not interested in hearing how they have planned and implemented their event and that I want to see how well they have understood how to manage a project. But they still do it. Why? Because it's their comfort zone.

But getting it wrong has consequences, as you will see.

We're going to look at each of the different quadrants in a moment but first a word about events in general. Make no mistake, every event, from the smallest meeting to an international blockbuster, is a piece of theatre. And at their heart, they are all about how they make you feel.

When I design a conference, for example, I follow the tried-and-tested rhythm of a musical. We begin with an animation set to music, an overture if you like. It tells the audience that we are about to begin and builds the excitement.

Then our first speaker is always rock solid. Just like the opening number in a musical, we are setting the scene. It tells the audience that they should feel safe in the knowledge that the event is going to be every bit as good as they have anticipated it being and that they are in for a good time.

Then over the course of the next few hours, the audience is entertained by speakers that teach, that motivate, that inspire. There is a definite rhythm to it. My team has got to the point where they try to guess which speaker is going to make the audience cry. By taking the audience on an emotional journey, they feel they have experienced something special. We add plenty of breaks for networking so they can talk about which bits they have liked best so far and to remind each other about things they have learned. And the final act is always someone who is so inspiring that they get a standing ovation, before the audience leaves the auditorium to go and dress to impress and celebrate the learning journey they have just been on.

Let's look at another type of event. What about that quarterly meeting where they go through all the figures with you? What is the purpose of that meeting? Well, it's not to bore you to death or to impart the figures. What's at the heart of that meeting is either a short, sharp shock that makes you feel that the company has not done as well as it should have done in the last quarter and that everyone needs to buck up their ideas for the rest of the year, or it's to celebrate how successful you have been, and to encourage you to do more of the same.

Think for a moment about an amazing event that you have attended. What made it so amazing? It might be a wedding, or a corporate event, or a party. Chances are, if its memorable, that will be because they paid attention to the detail. One of the best events that I went to was a wedding where every element had been thought through in minute detail to ensure that everyone left feeling loved and important. Everything had been thought through, from catering for everyone's individual tastes to heel covers so the ladies didn't ruin the heels of their very expensive shoes when they walked across the lawn to take their seats for the wedding ceremony. That's what we should be aiming for. When we put on an event, we want to think about our attendee's experience from the first touch point all the way through to the last touch point, and make every step along the path as excellent as it can possibly be.

Conversely, think of an event that you attended that was horrible. Usually this will be because the detail wasn't thought through or because the organizers hadn't taken time to really understand the event's purpose.

Which brings us on to the first of our quadrants.

Understanding

Before we go any further, I want to talk about RACI.

FIGURE 10.2   RACI project management responsibilities model

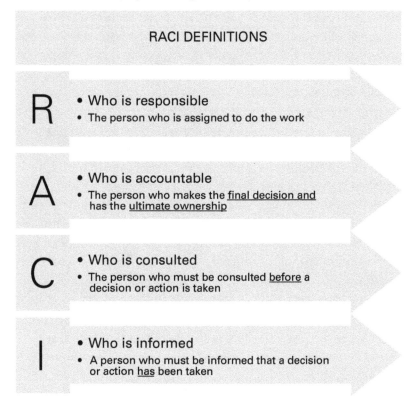

RACI DEFINITIONS

R
- Who is responsible
- The person who is assigned to do the work

A
- Who is accountable
- The person who makes the <u>final decision and</u> has the <u>ultimate ownership</u>

C
- Who is consulted
- The person who must be consulted <u>before</u> a decision or action is taken

I
- Who is informed
- A person who must be informed that a decision or action <u>has</u> been taken

In your case, the R, or the person who is responsible and is assigned to do the work, is you. You are managing the project.

The A, or the person who is accountable, is your manager or the person you are reporting to on this project.

The C, or people who need to be consulted, is anyone directly involved in the project, be that colleagues working on the project with you, other departments that will be affected or suppliers.

And finally, the I, or people who need to be kept informed, are those on the periphery. I often find that these people are the most troublesome. They want to know what's going on, but are not kept in the loop because they are not seen as a priority. Ignore them at your peril. Everything will run far more smoothly if you pander to their need for information.

I mention RACI here because your first step is to understand the roles that people will play and what your resource is in terms of people, time and budget.

People love to be involved in events. They put their hands up pretty quickly to be part of the team. But as the event gets nearer, you will find they may drop off the radar or become too busy. Ensuring your project team understand from the beginning that if they are involved then this is a commitment will help keep them on track.

I would begin by asking lots of questions of the person who is accountable to ensure you understand their vision for this event and what they are trying to achieve. The aim at the end of this questioning is to be able to set some SMART goals and start preparing the action plan. A reminder that SMART stands for SPECIFIC, MEASURABLE, ACTION ORIENTED, REALISTIC and TIME-LIMITED.

Going back to our chapter on strategy (Chapter 7), your questions should be the open-ended ones, to ensure you are extracting the most information – how, what, where, when, which, who and of course, why. As ever, the why is the most important.

The questions are probably the most important part of the process when it comes to understanding. My favourite question to ask a client when I am organizing an event for them is, 'If this event was to be wildly successful and everything about it was just about as good as you could possibly imagine, what would that look like?' It opens the doors for them to tell you their vision.

I would want to understand who it is aimed at. Who is my audience? What is their demographic? What do I want attendees to remember most about the event? Can you summarize the experiences our attendees should have?

Do you understand why people are going to want to attend? What's in it for them? How do we want them to feel as they walk away from the event? If you could describe the vibe of the event in 10 words, what would they be? This is to help with marketing – and don't forget that internal events still need marketing. There is nothing worse than sitting at an event not knowing why you are there.

Then, what are they trying to achieve? What do they want the end result to be? This question is really useful for measuring the outcome and helps you to determine the success of the event. For example, supposing they say they want to improve morale. When you put together the feedback form at the end, one of the questions in that feedback form should be, 'One of the goals of this event was to improve morale. Do you feel it achieved this?' As long as they answer 'Yes', job done and goal achieved.

The answers to these questions are going to help you get the right feel for your event, determine what the right venue is, decide what the programme will be and get a feel for any extras you might need in the budget.

It's worth looking at this point to see whether this event has ever been done before and if so, whether you have a file that contains all the details of what happened last time. If the project manager did their job properly, you should have details of supplier communication and their contact details, the budget, a debrief document and a summary of the attendee feedback. There is no point in reinventing the wheel if you don't have to and if this document is available, it's a great starting point.

So now you understand what you are trying to achieve, we want to move into quadrant two.

Planning

Planning falls into three parameters:

Cost – the budget
Quality – the specification
Time – the schedule

All three of these will have an impact on each other when you change something. For example, if your manager wants an event in two weeks' time, both the quality and the cost will be impacted because you won't have time to organize it properly unless you throw lots of money at it, and even then, you won't have the time you need to organize it in as much detail as you would like.

Or supposing your manager tells you that you only have £20 a head to spend. The quality of the event and the schedule will be affected, because it's going to take a lot longer to find a venue at that cost and to negotiate.

So, if you change one of the above, you'd better look at all three and you're going to need to track all three parameters as you proceed.

Let's start with the budget. What is a budget? Obviously, it's a spreadsheet that tracks the income and expenditure of your event, but it's also a checklist for your event and a great way to manage it. I always manage my events from my budget.

There are two ways in which to build a budget.

The first is a bottom-up budget. This is where they tell you what they are trying to achieve, and you have free rein to create the perfect event specification. The second is top down. This is where management decides what is to be spent and you create the event to fit that budget. You might have to compromise on some of the things that you want to do, but I would always prefer to operate this way. In my experience, when you are asked to put together a bottom-up budget, you do all the work of collating the information and when you present it, they say, 'Oh that's a lot more than I thought it would be. Please work within XYZ budget.' At the very least, I would try to tie them down to a rough idea of what spend they have in mind before you embark on putting a plan into place. Ask, 'I know you said there is an unlimited budget but roughly what does that look like? Is it £20–£30k? More? Less?'

Before you can start work on your budget you will first need to put the specification in place. Until you have scoped and designed the event it's impossible to budget it.

I have created a budget sheet that has every element on it that I could possibly spend money on, and from that I decide what I want to include in this event, so I don't miss anything. In events, checklists are your best friend, and I also have a template that I customize at the start of any event project that I undertake.

On the budget I include every element that I can think of. I have nine categories:

- Rooms
- Transportation
- Food and beverage
- Audiovisual
- Printed materials
- Administration
- Recreation
- Speaker fees
- Miscellaneous

Within each category, I look for every possible associated expense, including all taxes, gratuities, insurances, security, credit card fees and incidentals, such as golf club rentals.

You only get stung once and then you check everything. In Europe, budgeting is much easier than in the US. We have a DDR or Daily Delegate Rate which includes everything we will be spending, with the exception of AV. It's worked out per person so it's nice and easy. If you have 70 people, you multiply the DDR by 70 and there is your cost. In Europe, you are also able to book hotel rooms and give them back if they don't get booked by your delegates.

Not so in the States where booking events seems to be a game of trying to hide as many expenses as possible until the last moment, to get you to spend far more than you thought. Every tiny element is charged separately and the contracts are so complicated you need a master's to understand them. I have never understood this way of working. It's irritating at best, but as a smaller company, to suddenly be told on the day of a conference that internet isn't included and that is a further $5,000 or that taxes and gratuities were not included and that they are another 38 per cent on top of what you have budgeted for is highly stressful. Transparency makes for a far better experience for both parties. These days, I tell venues that when I sign the contract, that is what I will be budgeting for and so they had better make sure everything is included in that contract. I don't want any surprises.

I also always budget 10 per cent as a contingency. This is because there is always something unexpected that needs paying for at the last minute. A speaker may have forgotten their workbooks for example and need them printing.

You can see from the graphic how to organize your spreadsheet so that you can use your budget to manage your event.

In the income and expenditure column you will first list all the ways in which you will get revenue, for example ticket sales, sponsorships, tours, dinners, etc.

And then you will list all the things that are costs, in minute detail, by category. If you've never done a budget like this before, it's well worth brainstorming what you want to include with your project team. You'll be far less likely to miss anything.

Your second column is labelled 'Projected' and in it, you will put your best guestimate for what the income and costs are

FIGURE 10.3 Project budget example

	Income and Expenditure	Projected	Actual	Variance	Timing	Supplier/Contact	Notes
35	*Food and Beverage*						
36	Friday Dinner						
37	DDR main conference						
38	Gala Dinner						
39	Wine						
40	Drinks and Canape reception						
41	Speakers' Dinner						
42	Gratuities						
43	*Audiovisual*						
44	Set labour, partitions, risers						
45	Partitions						
46	Risers						
47	AV (in-house contractor)						
48	Signs, monitors, headers						
49	Telephone/fax/electronic communications						
50	Lighting/staging/labour (don't forget rehearsals)						
51	Security						
52	Cleaning						
53	Flipcharts, easels, chalkboard rentals						
54	Electrical power, electricians						
55	Pipe and drape for exhibits, displays						

likely to be for each item. This is where having historical data will come in particularly useful as it will paint a clear picture of what happened last time and what expectations for revenue and costs are.

The next column is 'Actual' and as you confirm what your costs will be with your suppliers, these go here. Our sales team sends me figures on a weekly basis so I can update our revenues.

The 'Variance' column is, in my opinion, the most important column on the spreadsheet when it comes to managing your project through the budget. If you can see that the budget variance is showing that you are making less profit than you had forecast, you know you are going to have to shave off some of the costs.

There are always things in the budget that are 'imperative must-haves', and then there are 'nice-to-haves'. The imperatives obviously have to be accounted for, but the nice-to-haves can be dropped if you don't have enough money to hit your forecast. However, it's worth remembering that the nice-to-haves are the details that people will comment on and remember. They are what makes your event stand out from the rest, so you want to use polite but firm negotiation tactics to keep costs down so that you have budget to include these in the final event. Keep your eye on this column and manage it to within an inch of your life and you can't go wrong.

Our next column is 'Timing' and in this column I put when the element needs to be in place by, and when we need to start working on it. Just the month, but it helps when I come to draw up the timeline later on.

Next to that is the 'Supplier/Contractor' column into which I put which supplier or contractor is dealing with each element, along with their contact details. Not only is this incredibly useful when it comes to having all the contact details close at hand, but next time you come to manage this event, all the historic data including contacts will be there.

And finally there is a 'Notes' column in case there is anything I want to ensure I have clarity on. For example, supposing I have a cost for a networking event in the budget. It might be worth noting that this cost was for 75 people, so that next time we know how much it cost per head.

Your budget is a living, breathing document. I visit and update mine on a daily basis. That way I am always on top of the figures. In the week of the run-up to the event, there are always costs that appear from nowhere. Be sure to add them into the budget so you don't forget them next time.

Strong negotiation skills are a must as a project manager and businesses expect it. I learned a great lesson when I ran my Executive Support LIVE event. As part of my negotiation, I had allowed the venue to write an article on how to work best with a hotel. In that article, the author explained that when they quote you, they expect you to negotiate. It's a starting point for a discussion. And when you just accept the quote without further discussion, they do a happy dance, because now they are a lot closer to their target than they thought they would be.

If you want something, ask for it – they can only say no. Remember if you negotiate before the contract is signed, it's called negotiating. If you negotiate after the contract is signed, it's called begging. It's better to be a good negotiator than an expert beggar.

Everything is negotiable but everything also has a price. Remember that quoted prices are invitations to buy, but not statements of value.

To negotiate well you need to understand what you have in your armoury that has a perceived value but which costs you nothing or almost nothing that you can use to negotiate costs down.

Here are a few examples:

- agreeing to add the venue and hotel to your preferred suppliers list

- agreeing to hold a dinner at the venue as well as the main event
- agreeing to allow someone from the venue to welcome everyone
- giving them a free booth from which to market their venue
- putting their marketing material in the goody bags
- organizing a show-around for anyone that wants it
- organizing a free drinks reception in a part of the venue that they particularly want to showcase to your audience
- agreeing to come back the following year with the same event or host other events there over the course of the next 12 months

As you can see, none of the above cost anything, but for the venue there is a real value in negotiating like this so that you both come out of it feeling like you have won. Remember the relationship. When you have finished negotiating, you are going to have to work with these people, so negotiate hard but always remain polite and professional.

And always negotiate at the proper authority level. There is nothing worse than feeling like you have done an amazing piece of negotiation, only for the person you are negotiating with to say that they need to check with their superiors.

Another tip that came from that same article, by the way, was to not have too much food choice. When you offer lots of different options, people feel compelled to take a little piece of everything, so the queue for lunch will be long and slow. Fewer food options will mean the line moving far faster. And ask the chef what other events they have going on at the venue, and what their food choices are. Sometimes, if you choose the exact same food options, they will offer a discount because they now only have to prepare a larger quantity of the same menu instead of two different selections.

Let's talk about your venue in a little more detail. What is the atmosphere that you want from your venue? Does the venue you are looking at fit with your audience and event goals? What facilities does it have and are any of them things you can add into your event package or present as features? For example, we often negotiate with the hotel spa to provide a special rate or package for our delegates.

Another hotel we worked with had a wing that was entirely for the use of female customers. They had additional security for that wing and every room had some nice additional touches, like a pair of GHD hair straighteners. We would have been crazy not to have included these benefits in our marketing.

We also work with the venue in other ways. For example, we help them to craft social media messages to go out over the course of the event which raise the awareness of their brand with our audience by including messaging and hashtags that engage them. They usually provide us with at least one prize for our charity auction, which is great branding for them. Most hotels will have relationships with some local tourist attractions and tour operators, so we work with the hotel to recommend these to our guests, which helps them and us. And we offer the assistants of any of the businesses that they have on their database a discount on tickets. Again, this is a win-win. They have something of value to offer their clients, they can shout about the fact that we are hosting our conference with them, and we sell more tickets.

Other things to consider:

- Is the room size right and does it have high ceilings? You don't want to feel cramped and claustrophobic.
- Does it have natural light? A full day is a long time to be sat in an enclosed space with no windows.
- Are there enough breakout rooms?
- Is it easy to get to by most forms of public transport? I've visited many venues in my time that are stunning but have rejected them because getting to them is too hard.

- And most importantly, does the venue reflect your company brand?

We talked about the devil being in the detail earlier in the chapter, but it all boils down to thinking about every eventuality and being considerate. Have you thought about how you will handle specific dietary requirements? Does the venue have facilities for people with disabilities? Are guests bringing partners? Why not set up some activities to keep them entertained while business presentations are going on?

If you ask all the relevant questions well in advance, you can cater for everyone.

But you also need to be prepared for things that could go wrong and make sure there are contingency plans in place. Here are a few tips.

- Check that the venue has no renovation works scheduled.
- If all your attendees are travelling together, what will you do if there is a delay en route?
- Allow plenty of time for presentation run-throughs and for testing equipment – and have access to at least basic replacement equipment if anything breaks down.
- If your event clashes with something that's likely to draw huge crowds or strain local resources, consider revising your timetable – get your guests in earlier, for example.
- Finally, make sure you have everyone's contact details, and they have yours – and keep your mobile phone charged.

Now you know what you are trying to achieve, and you have an outline of the event, you will need to put some timelines in place. Begin by breaking down the overall objectives into specific tasks, and then identify who is responsible for which task, and by when. Your work schedule needs to include estimated timelines. You should include start and finish times. Some tasks can be done concurrently, and some will need to be done sequentially.

You will need to keep checking back to ensure individual goals are met as they have a tendency to slip. And build in contingency time. It always takes longer than you think to get stuff done.

My tip for this part of the planning is that once you are done, you should pull the project team together to look at and approve it. Otherwise, when things DO slip, and they will, they will tell you that they didn't agree to those timelines and that they were unrealistic. Getting them to approve them creates buy-in and accountability.

Back in the dark ages, before computers, when I first started organizing events, we used to use Post-it notes for planning our events. It meant that we could spend a few hours brainstorming and sticking every step of the event to the wall in the most minute detail.

Then we would allocate tasks to people, put them in timeline order and add deadlines so everyone knew where they were. But it also had another very practical purpose. It meant I had visibility. As people came and removed their tasks as they did them, I was able to see whether we were on track to deliver on time or whether we had a problem. I could clearly see whether we were doing well when lots of the Post-its had disappeared, or whether I needed to chase people because the wall was still full of notes.

The best project management systems will give you this visibility. I particularly like Trello. It's really simple. But it is the modern version of the Post-its. We have three columns: red for 'not started yet', yellow for 'working on' and green for 'completed'. You can allocate tasks to people and set deadlines on it too. And it will let you know when tasks are late. Microsoft Planner, which is part of Teams, does something similar, although it's not colour coded in the same way. But I can clearly see exactly where we are with each task.

The goal is that you all work together as a team and you are going to be far more successful at that if you schedule reviews at fixed times right from the beginning so everyone knows when the check-in dates are and by when they will be held to account if tasks aren't done. It also means that if things start to go awry, they can be reined back in before they become too much of a problem.

You are going to play a number of roles in this review process: listener, contributor and leader.

Your event plan and your budget are your shopping list. Take time to put it together properly in the beginning and you'll save time – and probably money – in the long term. So, focus on the nitty gritty as well as the big picture – the more detail the better. You'll be pleased you took time to do it later on.

You will need to keep comprehensive records of your event plan too. Project managing your event will require observation, communication and documentation. Good documentation will ensure that your event runs smoothly. You can use it alongside your people skills to solve problems.

I much prefer a physical file, but then I am from a generation that always worked that way. If you prefer an online file then, of course, I have no problem with that. Whatever works for you!

For me, as much as I have embraced tech, if there is an emergency and my heart is pounding, it is easier to find things in a paper format. For example, we once had a delegate that had such a bad nut allergy that even a hint of contact could have sent her into anaphylactic shock. We had written to the hotel before our event to alert them to the fact. About 10 minutes before the afternoon break, Matt messaged me in a state of great alarm. The afternoon snacks had been put out and it was a nut fest. There were even small bowls of nuts. He had tried explaining but they were swearing blind that they hadn't been informed. Because my file was so organized, I was able to lay my hands on a print-out of the email confirmation from the hotel in quite literally a few seconds. The nuts were removed, a different tea appeared, and everything returned to normal. I am not sure whether I would have been able to lay my hands on what I needed quite as quickly if I had needed to do so electronically. I think my brain would have been in overdrive and unable to think clearly. And my hands were shaking so much, I don't know how I would have used my phone.

Your file should be so comprehensive that if you were suddenly taken sick, your colleagues should be able to pick up your event and run with it. In 2018, my son was taken ill and my team and the other speakers were able to seamlessly carry on with the event as if I had been there so that it was delivered in the way that I wanted it to be. It's the only event of my own that I have ever missed, but it helped that I knew they had got it.

The file should include:

- your project plan, clearly marked up to show what you still need to do and what has already been done
- your budget
- pertinent emails from your suppliers
- all the contact details for the venue, your suppliers, the speakers and your team
- a list of delegates with contact details and which parts of the event they are attending
- a full running order for the entire event, including a minute-by-minute production schedule

Implementing

So now the Understanding and Planning parts are done, it's time to Implement the plan. And if you've done all the work properly, that will be really easy.

An event manager usually starts as a planner and organizer and then shifts gear at implementation to become a communicator and problem solver. You simply have to follow and direct the plan.

Here are a few tips for the implementation.

Firstly, use human instead of paper signage. It's more to have people welcoming guests and handing them off to the next person in the chain. It's part of the customer journey that we talked about earlier, making sure that every step of the process contributes to how they feel.

Badges need to be thought through before you order and print them. In my experience, they always seem to be hanging in the wrong place, so I can't see the names properly and end up looking at somebody's cleavage. The best badges that I have seen have the first name in very large letters and ideally a logo as well as a company name so you can instantly see where they're from. And of course, they should always be laid out at the event in alphabetical order so you can find them easily for your attendees as they arrive. There are companies that will not only print your badges for you, but will also deliver them already in alphabetical order. It's money well spent.

When I invite speakers to take part in my conferences, and they are speaking on my stage, I almost feel that my role is that of a dinner party host, introducing interesting people to each other. And so it would go totally against the grain to then be interrupted every five minutes by members of my team that need questions answered. To avoid this scenario, we always set up a WhatsApp group so that the team and I are able to communicate throughout the event without the need for them to physically come and ask me questions.

Don't forget to hire a photographer. Whether the event is internal or external, you should have a set list of photos that you need taking for marketing purposes later. We often forget this when it's an internal event but photos of people having a great time are always a good idea for when you come to market the event again next year.

And finally, hiring a professional AV (audio visual) company will be one of the best decisions you ever make. Twenty-five years ago, when I first worked with Emma Reynolds, who handles all my production, she told me not to worry about what happens on stage because she has got that. She has never let me down, and it's a huge bonus knowing that if we have done our job and got that understanding and planning part right, she will make sure that translates to what needs to happen on stage.

Completing

So, what happens now? The event is done, and it was a huge success. There is a tendency to want to high-five and celebrate that it is done and that it went off well. But you're not done yet. You still have to Complete the event and that means tying up all the loose ends.

The budget needs completing and all those bills that suddenly appeared in the last week need to be added into the 'Actual' column so we don't forget them and can forecast properly next time.

You need copies of all the supplier invoices, and they need to be sent to accounts for their records and to be paid.

You need to send out a feedback form, to look at what the audience enjoyed or didn't so you can improve next time. Don't forget to include questions that will prove to your manager that the event delivered exactly what they wanted it to. What was the ROI (return on investment)? Don't forget that the evaluation is not just about hard facts but also the soft options; for example, how did it make them feel?

And then the project team should sit down as a group, no longer than a week after the event, to do a debrief whilst it's still fresh in their heads. The purpose is to look at what worked and what could have been done better, but this is not a finger-pointing exercise. Rather it's a learning opportunity so that the next event is even more spectacular. It's a 'we' exercise. It means that the next time, we'll start the event with a baseline and evaluation.

All this information needs to go onto the top of your file so that you have a complete history and record of this event for future use.

And finally, enjoy it! You'll probably never have worked so hard in your life, but when it's a huge success it will be you and the team that get the glory.

Reference

Association for Project Management (2019) *Body of Knowledge*, 7th Edition, Association for Project Management

CHAPTER ELEVEN

The problem is not the problem

As an administrative professional, problem solving is a key part of your job. Why? Because it's another core part of saving your manager time.

As Captain Jack Sparrow so eloquently put it, 'The problem is not the problem. The problem is your attitude about the problem.'

When I first employed Matt, he used to come to me and tell me we had a problem. He would relay what the problem was and I would ask him to leave it with me. A large part of my job was solving problems. So much so, that a lot of my other work stacked up. I seemed to spend most of my life firefighting.

And then I read a management book called *The One Minute Manager Meets the Monkey* by Ken Blanchard.

The book focuses on effective time management and delegation. It uses a metaphor of monkeys representing tasks and responsibilities that should be delegated appropriately to team members rather than being held onto by the manager. The central idea is that managers should not allow their staff to transfer their problems onto them but rather guide them to take responsibility and solve their own problems.

It explained that some problems are huge gorillas, whereas others are marmosets, but by saying 'leave it with me', as a manager, you take all of the responsibility on yourself, which is not the best use of your time. Not only that, but you also don't allow anyone else to learn how to solve problems. The secret, the book said, was to ask, 'What do you think? How would you solve it?' and so empowering your team to think for themselves.

By the time we were done, Matt would come to me not just with the problem but with a history of the facts behind the problem and several possible solutions. This freed up huge amounts of my time, because I could make an informed decision quickly.

However, when it comes to problem solving, it's not as straightforward as you might think. You should be aware that there are several stumbling blocks.

Firstly, we often fail to recognize the ACTUAL problem. We are so keen to come up with a solution that we see the problem at a surface level rather than digging deeper to clarify what is at the root of the problem.

For example, imagine your manager is frequently missing deadlines and not completing their tasks on time. You assume the problem is poor time management skills, so you send out reminders and chase them constantly. However, despite these efforts, the manager continues to miss deadlines and struggles to complete their tasks on time.

You failed to see that the real problem was with the workflow and process in place. The manager was not given clear guidelines and expectations for their tasks by their line manager, resulting in confusion and delays.

In this case, you failed to identify the root cause of the problem and instead focused on a symptom of the problem. This led to wasted resources and a delay in solving the real problem.

Another block to effective problem solving is conceiving the problem too narrowly.

An executive assistant manages their manager's calendar and schedules appointments. The assistant receives a request from a potential client for a meeting, but the only available time slots are during her executive's lunch break or after work hours. The assistant assumes that the problem is finding a time for the meeting and informs the potential client that the meeting is not possible at this time.

However, the assistant failed to recognize that the potential client may have been willing to meet over lunch or after work hours, and the real problem was with the assistant's assumption that these times were unacceptable. The assistant may have overlooked the importance of accommodating potential clients' schedules and could have missed out on a valuable business opportunity.

In this case, the assistant conceived the problem too narrowly and failed to consider alternative solutions that could have met both the boss' and the potential client's needs. This led to missed opportunities and a potential loss of business.

Another barrier is reacting emotionally.

An administrative assistant receives a critical email from a colleague who is upset about a mistake made on a project. The assistant becomes defensive and emotional, responding by sending a strongly worded email, blaming the colleague for not providing enough information and accusing them of being unreasonable.

In this scenario, the administrative assistant reacted emotionally when problem solving. By becoming defensive and blaming the colleague, the assistant failed to objectively assess the situation and find a solution to the problem. This emotional reaction may have further escalated the situation, damaged the relationship with the colleague and delayed finding a solution to the mistake made on the project.

In problem solving, remaining calm and objective is important, even when faced with criticism or challenging situations. Emotional reactions can cloud judgment and make finding a solution to the problem at hand more difficult. Instead, take a step back, evaluate the situation and respond in a professional manner that focuses on finding a solution to the problem.

What about a scenario where we make hasty choices without considering all the options?

An administrative assistant is responsible for managing a project timeline and discovers that a task is behind schedule. The assistant immediately assumes that the only solution is to work overtime and pushes team members to work extra hours to complete the task, without considering alternative options.

In this scenario, the assistant made a hasty choice without looking at the options when problem solving. The assistant failed to consider alternative solutions, such as delegating tasks to other team members, rearranging the schedule or negotiating a new deadline with stakeholders. By jumping to the conclusion that the only solution was to work overtime, the assistant may have created an unnecessary burden on team members, resulting in lower-quality work, burnout and decreased morale.

In problem solving, it's important to take the time to evaluate all the options and weigh the pros and cons before making a decision. Hasty choices can lead to unintended consequences and may not address the root cause of the problem. Take a step back, gather information, consider the alternatives and make an informed decision that is in the best interest of the project and the team.

You also need to look at all of the possible consequences of your decision.

An administrative assistant is responsible for managing the budget for a project. The assistant identifies an opportunity to save money by purchasing cheaper supplies from a new vendor. The assistant fails to consider the consequences of this decision, such as the quality of the supplies, the reliability of the vendor and the impact on the project timeline.

As a result, the assistant makes the purchase, but the supplies turn out to be of poor quality, causing delays in the project and additional costs for replacement. The vendor also turns out to be unreliable, causing further delays and additional expenses.

In this scenario, the assistant failed to consider all the consequences when problem solving. While the decision to save money was important, the assistant failed to consider the potential risks and trade-offs of this decision. This led to negative consequences for the project and additional costs, ultimately outweighing the potential savings.

In problem solving, it's important to look at all the potential consequences of a decision before making a choice. Consider the risks, trade-offs and unintended consequences, and weigh them against the potential benefits. This can help ensure that the decision is best for the project and the organization.

And finally we sometimes fail to consider the feasibility of the solution.

An administrative assistant is responsible for managing the inventory of office supplies. The assistant notices that paper products are frequently running out, causing delays and disruptions in the workplace. The assistant suggests that the company stockpile more paper products to prevent future shortages without considering the feasibility of this solution.

Upon further investigation, the assistant discovers that the storage space in the office is limited, and stockpiling paper products would require costly renovations or the use of expensive off-site storage facilities. In this scenario, the assistant failed to consider the feasibility of the solution proposed to solve the problem.

In problem solving, it's important to evaluate the feasibility of the proposed solution, considering factors such as available resources, time constraints and cost. Failure to consider feasibility can lead to impractical or costly solutions that may not solve the problem effectively. Evaluating all aspects of a potential solution before implementing it is important.

Here are a couple of structured ways to solve problems effectively so you don't encounter the barriers above.

The first is the traditional method and how I was taught to do it at the beginning of my career. It still has its benefits and is the way many of the companies I have worked for and with still like to structure their problem solving.

The traditional method

1 You should begin by clarifying exactly what the problem is that you are facing. Be specific and objective about it.

2 Gather information: once you have identified the problem, gather all the necessary information related to the problem. This may include data, reports and feedback from colleagues or clients.

3 Analyse the information: once you have all the information, you should analyse it. Review the information you have gathered and try to identify patterns or potential causes of the problem.

4 Generate possible solutions: brainstorm possible solutions to the problem. Be creative and consider all options.

5 Evaluate the solutions: evaluate each possible solution and consider its pros and cons. Determine which solution is the most feasible and effective.

6 Implement the solution: once you have identified the best solution, take action to implement it. Assign tasks to team members, set deadlines and monitor progress.

7 Monitor the solution's implementation and effectiveness. Adjust as necessary and continue monitoring the situation to ensure the problem does not reoccur.

8 Remember, effective problem solving requires critical thinking, communication and collaboration with others. Involve other team members or stakeholders as needed to ensure the best possible outcome.

I followed this structure for years and whilst it was very effective, about 10 years ago, I came across another, much more creative way of problem solving and I have used it ever since.

The Six Thinking Hats

The Six Thinking Hats method is a problem-solving technique developed by Edward De Bono that encourages individuals to approach problems from different perspectives. Each 'hat' represents a different perspective or mode of thinking, and the goal is to use each hat to consider the problem from all angles.

It enables me to think in a broader way, making my problem solving far more effective. I love it because it involves role playing. If you play the role of someone whose job it is to be negative, for example, nobody will get upset if you come up with all the negative reasons why a solution won't work. It's simply your role.

By encouraging creative, parallel and lateral thinking, it improves communication and speeds up decision making because it avoids debate based on emotion or ego.

When I talk about the six hats in my class, I get everyone into groups of six, and each delegate takes on the role of a different hat to solve three problems. But of course, in real life, this would usually not be appropriate or possible, so I simply think through each of the hats in turn, to ensure I have considered possible solutions from all angles.

Here's how you can apply the Six Thinking Hats method to problem solving for assistants.

There are six different hats and you want to tackle them in this order.

1 **Blue Hat:** This hat represents control and organization. The person who takes on this hat manages the thinking process and guides the discussion. They think about the next steps and how to implement the solution and make the final decision as to what the solution will be. The Blue Hat sets the agenda, suggests the next steps, asks for feedback from the other hats, asks for summaries, draws conclusions and makes decisions.

2 **White Hat:** This hat represents data and information. If you are the white hat, you should gather all relevant information and data related to the problem you are trying to solve. Use this information to analyse the problem objectively and identify any missing information that needs to be acquired. The White Hat will ask, 'What information do we have here?', 'What information is missing?', 'What information would we like to have?' and 'How are we going to get the information?'.

3 **Green Hat:** This hat represents creativity and innovation. Whoever plays this hat's role has to work out potential solutions. They should be encouraged to think outside the box and consider unconventional solutions as well as those that are obvious. Green hats want to know, 'What are some possible solutions and courses of action?', 'Are there any additional alternatives?', 'Could we do this in a different way?', 'Could there be another explanation?'.

4 **Red Hat:** This hat represents emotions and feelings. This role involves considering how the problem and the possible solutions will affect you and others involved. How will they make you and others feel? Consider any potential negative or positive consequences that may arise from the solution. Red hats tend to say things like, 'My gut feeling is that this will work out beautifully', 'I don't like the way this is being done',

'This proposal is going to really upset people', 'My intuition tells me that this will cause us problems'.

5 **Black Hat:** This hat represents caution and criticism. The role of this hat is to identify potential problems or issues that may arise from the solution. Think about potential obstacles and drawbacks that may affect the success of the solution. They will look at the weaknesses and why it won't work.

6 **Yellow Hat:** This hat represents optimism and positivity. Whoever gets this hat should identify the benefits and positive outcomes that may arise from the solution and think about how the solution may improve the situation. They look at why it will work and why they love it as a solution.

Can you see how it will work? It's a great way to think your way around problems from every angle. These days when I get presented with a problem, I immediately think, what are the facts? Is there a contract? Is there an email trail?

Then I look at possible solutions before looking at how my solutions will make people feel, and what the negative and positive impacts might be before finally making a decision.

By using the Six Thinking Hats method, you can approach problem solving with a holistic and comprehensive perspective. This technique encourages critical thinking, creativity and collaboration, making it an effective tool for assistants in solving complex problems.

Whichever method you choose, problem solving is a crucial skill because you deal with a variety of complex and dynamic situations in your day-to-day work. As an assistant, you will encounter problems or challenges that require quick thinking, creative solutions and effective decision-making skills. Solving problems efficiently and effectively can help you save time and resources – not only for you but also for your manager. This helps minimize risks and ensures that tasks and projects are completed successfully.

Moreover, you are expected to support your manager or team in achieving their goals and objectives as an assistant. This means that you need to be able to anticipate potential obstacles or challenges that may arise and proactively find ways to overcome them. By being a good problem solver, you can anticipate issues and develop effective solutions before they become a problem.

Overall, problem solving is essential for your role because it enables you to work more effectively, efficiently and productively. By mastering this skill, you will add value to your role and become an even more indispensable member of your team.

References

Blanchard, K (1999) *The One Minute Manager Meets the Monkey*, William Morrow

De Bono, E (1986) *Six Thinking Hats*, Little Brown & Co

CHAPTER TWELVE

Stress: how to stop the overwhelm

It might seem strange to end on a chapter about stress, but I promise to send you away, dancing down the street, knowing that you can do anything.

Let's face it, the majority of assistants are permanently operating under stress, mainly because most managers have no idea how long things take to complete, how much things really cost to get done or how many nights you spend in the office juggling the workload to try to get everything back on track.

Is it any wonder that you are so stressed?

The profession is in an acute state of change and in the process of creating what the new strategic role looks like.

The press is reporting that the role is disappearing, which doesn't help our status within the organizations that we serve.

We have no clear career progression and are excluded from so much of what everyone else at our organizations takes for granted.

Add to that the ever-increasing number of people that we are expected to look after, with with the majority looking after four people.

And ever since Covid-19, we've been creating our new world of work and making it up as we go along, as well as trying to renegotiate the work-life balance we lost over those two years. It's no longer work-life balance that we are working with, it's work-life integration. A senior HR director told me recently that of 32 assistants on his watch, six are off on long-term sick leave, five have resigned and they are watching eight more. This is because over the period of Covid, everyone went into survival mode and senior partners started doing 12 meetings a day instead of eight. The assistants knuckled down and supported. They took no time off. Now we are emerging from the other side, nobody is quite sure how to push back to where they were before the pandemic.

Stress makes us feel various things: out of control, angry, depressed, exhausted and tearful are words that regularly make an appearance when I ask stressed delegates to explain how they're feeling.

The cost of stress to organizations is huge. When we are working in an unhealthy workplace and there is too much work-related stress, unhealthy lifestyle practices are more likely to kick in. The result is depression, short- and long-term disability, absenteeism, litigation and a high turnover of staff. Employee satisfaction and commitment go down and so productivity is down and costs are up. Not ideal for anyone. According to its 2021/2022 annual statistics report, the Health and Safety Executive (HSE, the UK's workplace regulator) reported that there were:

- an estimated 914,000 cases of work-related stress, depression or anxiety
- an estimated 17 million working days lost due to work-related stress, depression or anxiety

Meanwhile Zippia Research's 40+ Worrisome Workplace Stress Statistics (Mazur, 2023) show us that:

- 83 per cent of US workers suffer from work-related stress.
- US businesses lose up to $300 billion yearly as a result of workplace stress.
- Stress causes around 1 million workers to miss work every day.
- Only 43 per cent of US employees think their employers care about their work-life balance.
- Depression leads to $51 billion in costs due to absenteeism and $26 billion in treatment costs.
- Work-related stress causes 120,000 deaths and results in $190 billion in healthcare costs yearly.

There is such a thing as good stress though. We need enough stress to make sure that we don't get bored.

As you can see from Figure 12.1, when we have low stress and we also have low physical and mental activity we feel bored and frustrated. Our creativity and ability to motivate ourselves suffer. We don't want to remain constantly in our comfort zone. In order to feel like we are performing, we need to push ourselves into the optimal activity zone. The trick, though, is to learn to balance the two. If we are in the optimal activity zone for too long, we start to burn out. It's a little like sprinting in a race. We probably need to sprint to get over the finishing line, but if we do it for too long, we exhaust ourselves, we burn out and this leads to anxiety and low self-esteem. Same stress, different results, dependent on how hard we push ourselves and for how long.

The secret is to understand ourselves. When I got sick in 2012, I had been working ridiculous hours because it was year-end. I was on a train at 7 am and rarely home before 10 pm because I had a two-hour commute. I often arrived at work in the dark and left in the dark, never seeing daylight. I was drinking too much and smoking because by the time I got home, I needed to

FIGURE 12.1   Why we need a certain amount of stress to remain motivated

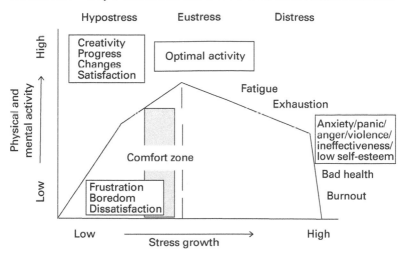

relax fast. I usually skipped lunch and as I said in an earlier chapter, my husband and I have seven children between us, so weekends didn't allow time to catch up. It was a recipe for disaster. As the founder of one of America's first department stores, John Wanamaker, apparently once said, 'People who cannot find time for recreation are obliged sooner or later to find time for illness.'

It's why I'm so passionate about making sure you are doing things that make your heart sing. I wasn't. Instead I was permanently exhausted and desperate to get off the hamster wheel.

These days I eat well, I sleep properly and I exercise regularly. These three things keep my stress at bay and my mind healthy.

As an assistant there are many things that contribute to our stress levels. The first is the oblivious manager. We've talked already about the fact that they often have no clue what your workload is like or how long things take. The problem is that when we continuously say yes to everything and don't push back, we become the go-to person for everything. I know why you do it. You are the problem solver. You pride yourself on getting things done. So when you say no, it goes against the grain. But it's not helpful to become a doormat.

You need to find your voice. If you are being asked to do something that will take an hour and are only given 30 minutes to do it, explain. Otherwise the work will either be substandard or late; either way, it doesn't reflect well on you. Likewise, if I ever asked Matt to do something for me and I asked him towards the end of the day, he would push back, ever so nicely, but he would say something to the effect of, 'How urgent is this, because it's going to take me a couple of hours to do. I am very happy to stay late to do it, but if it can be done tomorrow morning, do you mind if I do it first thing when I come in?' In this way, he let me know that he was happy to do it, but also made the amount of time the task would take clear. It helped us both with time management and prioritization. Remember, you are the expert at being the assistant, they are not. Manage expectations and you won't go wrong.

Let's talk about procrastination. All of us procrastinate in one way or another, but being successful as an assistant relies on an awareness of how often and how, so we can ensure that we are getting things done in a timely fashion.

The first type of procrastinator is the Perfectionist. If you fall under this category, you will most likely complete a piece of work, check it several times and then file it, just so you can check it again later to be sure it is 100 per cent right. There is far too much work to be done to be operating in this way. Sometimes, as Sheryl Sandberg, former COO of Facebook, says, 'Done is better than perfect', and these days, with apps like Grammarly available, check it by all means, but then send it. Get it off your plate.

Then there are the Dreamers. If you fall under this category, you will be given a piece of work to do and decide to think about the best way to do it. So you think about it in the shower, and on your way to and from work and during lunch, and you make some notes, and you talk to other people about it. And now the deadline is upon you and it's stressful. Timebox it. Get first the research and then the work done.

And what about the Worriers? Do you recognize this scenario? Someone brings you a piece of work and you ask them to leave it on your desk. And then you are so busy dealing with other work that you totally forget about it. A week later, you remember to look at it, but now you don't understand it – and you don't want to ask because that will let them know that now is the first time that you have looked at it. And it was due yesterday! Avoid the stress by checking every piece of work as it arrives so you can be sure you understand its importance and where it sits in the list of priorities so that you can timebox it.

When I worked for the big publishing company before my breakdown, I had 13 magazines and each magazine had 38 pages of budget. The EC wanted those re-forecast on a monthly basis so I suddenly became an accountant rather than a publisher. Figures are not my thing and although I could do it if I concentrated really hard, it was a grand old waste of time. It would have been far more helpful to have had a meeting with the accountant once a month to go through the budgets and make the necessary forecast changes. So, I used to think, surely to goodness, someone will realize what a total waste of my time and talent this is. I was a typical Defier, hoping that someone would rescue me before the dreaded process started again. But of course, they never did. And every month, I would be rushing at the last minute to complete them because I had put them off because I hated doing them so much. Remember what Mark Twain said about eating the frogs? In other words, if there is something you hate doing, get it done up front because then your day is only going to get better. And if you have two things you hate doing, do the worst one first.

Or maybe you are a Crisis Maker. Our research shows that over 40 per cent of you say that you work best under pressure. And that works, until you have six hours to do eight hours of work and you've suddenly been called into a meeting. Put it into the calendar. Allocate your time properly and get it done.

And finally, there's the Over-Giver. In other words, those of you who never say no. Your pile of work grows and grows as people know that if they ask you for something, you will always say yes. The problem with this is that you will still be stuck in the office at 8 pm whilst they skip out at 5. You need to learn to say no. We'll come onto that in a moment.

But first I want to talk to you about martyrdom and carrot soup.

I had been on a marathon trip to Australia and New Zealand and hadn't seen the children for over three weeks. They were still quite young. I landed in London and after 29 hours of travelling was exhausted.

A lady from the church called and asked whether at the weekend I might make a batch of carrot and coriander soup for an event they were holding for the homeless, and I very politely declined. However, she pushed the matter, saying lots of people were away and I was their last hope. And those poor homeless people looked forward to their monthly event so much. You get the picture.

So, I went to the local market and brought my body weight in carrots. By the time I was done, I was orange, my children were orange, my kitchen was orange and I never wanted to see another carrot again. The day arrived and I carried my huge pot of soup into the church kitchen, where, sitting on the stove already was a large pot of minestrone. Apparently the woman concerned had thought I sounded really tired and so had found someone else, but I had missed the voicemail.

A very wise person once said to me that it is better to feel uncomfortable for a few seconds than to be resentful for a longer period of time. So these days, I refuse to be a martyr. If someone asks me to do something and my head says no, I consider whether it will make me feel resentful and if it does, I say no.

Here are some things that assistants have told me over the years in class:

- I allowed social awkwardness to get in the way of saying no.
- I believed that 'I had to make this work'.
- I am meant to be the problem solver so I can't cause problems by saying no.
- They will be angry with me if I say no.
- They will think I am incapable of managing my time if I say no.

None of these are true. Saying 'no' to people can actually be good for your role, your mental health and your career. Can you think of anyone else who says yes all the time? When you say no, it tells people you value your time and that you know how to prioritize. I am a firm believer that we train people how to treat us. If you always say yes, it doesn't make you indispensable, it makes you a doormat.

There was a girl on a course I did quite recently who was obviously struggling. Whenever I teach about stress, there is always at least one person in the audience who is near to the edge. You can see them getting emotional and in this class, this girl was definitely feeling it.

So at the end of the class, I took her to one side and asked her about it. Turns out, she was the only assistant for 70 members of staff. She was a single mother, working late every night, she couldn't remember the last time she had taken a weekend off and not worked, and she hadn't taken vacation for a couple of years. Something had to give. She was well on her way to burnout.

I suggested that she did a time audit and looked at her sand and her stones (see Chapter 6) for a month, noting exactly how she was spending her time so that she could share it with her manager. She did so, and when she took it to him a month later, he was furious – not with her, but with all the other people who had been dumping their work on her.

Have you ever seen the film *Beetlejuice*? You know how when you say his name three times he suddenly appears and all sorts of mayhem ensues? Well, it's just like that. When you take on a job for someone else three times, psychologically it becomes yours. So be very careful. You can say yes twice and be helpful, but if you say yes for a third time, that task no longer belongs to them.

Anyway, he took all that work and gave it back to the people that were meant to be doing it and the last time that I heard from her, she sent me a postcard from Kenya, where she was away on safari with her daughter.

I have three tips for saying no.

The first is to separate the decision from the relationship. Saying yes or no should be about whether it's the right thing for you to be doing and not about the person who is asking you to do it.

Secondly, my whole mindset changed when I started thinking in terms of 'I choose to' instead of 'I have to'. It gave me back control and made me question whether I wanted to 'choose to'.

And finally, the shorter it is, the stronger it is. Saying no should be like ripping off a sticking plaster. Do it fast and it's far less painful.

One of my delegates recently reframed totally how I thought about saying no, and I love it. She said, 'Saying no is showing respect to the other person because it's not overcommitting yourself to something you can't deliver.'

So here are some great ways to say no and still look helpful:

- I understand you're under pressure, and I'd love to assist you. However, I'm currently working on a deadline for Lucy, and I don't have the spare capacity at the moment.
- I genuinely want to say yes, but it's not an area of expertise for me. Have you considered asking (insert name)? They might be better suited to help you.
- I'm happy to guide you on how to do that so that you can handle it yourself next time.

- I really wish I could help, but I have family commitments this evening and it's crucial for me to leave on time today.
- I'm currently occupied with preparing Lucy's board packs. However, if you could provide me with a longer lead time next time, I'll be able to prioritize and schedule it accordingly.
- Yes I can help, but it's not going to be until Thursday morning as I need to finish these reports before I start anything else (I particularly like this one because they only come to you when their hair is on fire and they need help now. In this response you are saying yes, but just not aligned to their deadline, so they are likely to go and find someone else to help instead).
- I can't right now, I'm sorry.

Remember, 'No' can be a complete sentence. You don't necessarily need to explain yourself.

I used to have a sign above my desk which said, 'Poor planning on your part does not constitute an emergency on mine!' In other words, I have my whole day planned out. It's timeboxed and I know what my priorities are. Why should I jump in and turn my work schedule upside down because you haven't planned yours properly? I am not of course suggesting that if you have time to spare you shouldn't jump in, but most of you tell me you are flat out, so why would you do this to yourself?

Another great source of stress is the number of times a day that you are interrupted, and this is a huge part of any assistant's job. According to time management figures published by dovico.com, many of us spend more than half of our working day being interrupted! The average number of times you get interrupted in a day is around 56 (Cole, 2004). And it takes a minimum of three minutes to get back into doing what you are doing, so that means you are spending three hours a day just being interrupted. Who has time for that?

As we already saw in the ABC/123 exercise in Chapter 8, getting rid of interruptions can give you up to 50 per cent of your time back. One assistant I talked to purchased a plant and told her colleagues that if the plant was on the desk, she was working on something and not to interrupt. Another brought all her fellow assistants 'Cones of concentration'; small traffic cones that served the same purpose as the plant. Yet another had three mugs that she drank out of. One was red, another yellow and the third green. If she was drinking from the red mug, you should only interrupt her under pain of death because she was working on something complicated that required attention; if she was drinking from the yellow cup, you could interrupt her if it was urgent; and if she was drinking from the green cup, you could interrupt her all day long. She did say, however, that whenever her manager wanted to interrupt her, he would pick up the green mug and go make her a cup of tea! My senior editor, Kathleen, regularly puts the Out of Office on when she is putting the magazine to bed, letting those trying to contact her know that she is on deadline and to not expect a response. She does, however, tell them if it is urgent then to call her.

Have you ever found yourself in a situation where the chaos is raining down all around you, and that's the moment you decide to create a new filing system, sort out all your photos, or clear out the inbox that is 90 per cent full? There is a reason for that. It's because when everything is out of control, your mind searches for something to control and put it into order. The phenomenon is real and the acronym for it is FEAR, or False Evidence Appearing Real. When we are panicked because of the stress of having too much to do, the feeling of danger appears real, even though it may have no real substance. It arises when we feel threatened or undermined, which makes us revert to the known and familiar. So, if you find yourself reorganizing every-thing, stop and take stock. Does this need doing right now or is it FEAR?

I want to return to Timeboxing again for a moment. It's going to be your best friend when it comes to managing your time because unlike the 'to-do' list, it keeps you honest. Where a 'to-do' list is overwhelming because of the sheer number of ever-increasing items on it, Timeboxing ensures we are concentrating on what we actually need to get done. We are not being busy fools, we are honing the stones we need to achieve today rather than keeping ourselves busy by tackling the sand; far more attractive as we get to cross far more things off our list.

Parkinson's Law comes into play here. Parkinson's Law says that work expands to fill the time allotted for its completion. So, if you set yourself time to complete a task, that is how long it will take you. As an example, I know of one entrepreneur who only works until 2 pm every day. Since he started his business 10 years ago he has always done this, and he is now worth over a billion dollars. He maintains that by treating each day like he is going on vacation tomorrow, he clears down the things he needs to do today and still manages to spend afternoons with his family. Imagine how freeing it is to have that kind of clarity around what you are needing to achieve.

What are your stones for the year ahead?

Make two lists – one for the work stones and one for the personal stones – and put them into your calendar before anything else. This should include vacation and personal development by the way as both are stones.

Now you can fit your sand and additional tasks around these important deadlines. And don't forget to add the work in quadrant four that we talked about in Chapter 7. Remember, the art of successful time management and planning is not just getting things done. It's getting the right things done at the right time.

Using Timeboxing will allow you to prioritize your to-do list and achieve this.

Timeboxing will also give you a comprehensive record of what you have done over the year so when you come to your annual review, you can easily look back at your achievements. In addition, you'll be building that shared calendar we talked about which allows you to communicate and collaborate more effectively. It will help you to feel more in control, particularly when it comes to interruptions and multitasking, allowing you to get more done in the time allotted so you aren't feeling so overwhelmed, creating feelings of achievement rather than doom.

You have to learn to protect the asset – you! It's a strange career. It's entirely based on you taking care of them, but if you don't take care of yourself, how are you going to hope to take care of them? You can't pour from an empty cup. And that involves making healthy choices both in a work environment and physically.

Food needs colour – you need to be eating a rainbow to get the nutrients you need. If you're eating brown food, it's probably not very good for you (I made that comment at Hershey when I trained there, and it didn't go down terribly well – true story!).

My idea of a great night out used to be to go partying until the early hours of the next day. I smoked, I drank and my exercise was dancing. These days my idea of a great night is to be home with a good book or out to dinner with friends. You can still find time for partying, but it's important to listen to your body clock. Going to bed at 9.30 occasionally isn't boring. It's great for your equilibrium, your skin and your brain.

And talking of exercise, I hate it. But I need it. My office at the other end of the seafront in Spain is almost exactly 10,000 steps to and from my apartment. Could I have rented one closer to home? Of course, but then I wouldn't have got my daily exercise and I would have been tempted to stay later or pop out to finish a piece of work. This way, my work-life balance is excellent. There is a reason that the top executives in the world exercise and have private chefs. It has as much to do with mental health as it does physical health. Running a business and a private life alongside it can be brutal unless you plan it proactively and understand that you are an asset to be protected and nurtured.

If you can't do these three things, for any reason, do the next best thing. For example, when I am away speaking at conferences, it's not always easy to eat as I would like, but I do my best to eat healthily – not too many carbs, no alcohol and lots of water.

Three further brief pointers that I live by that I hope will help:

- Your network is your net worth but there is a reason it's called net 'work' and not net 'play' – it is hard work to maintain a network that supports each other. Now is the time to develop your network, not when you need it.
- There is a power in detachment. It doesn't mean you don't care if you detach. When you are emotionally involved in everything, it saps the energy from the things you need to focus on.
- Focus on what you can control. There is no point in focusing on things you can't control because you can't do anything to influence the outcome. It's a waste of time and energy. It took me years to learn to do this, but when I did, it was a revelation and helped me to avoid enormous amounts of stress.

My husband always says, 'Today is the tomorrow that you worried about yesterday, and all is well.'

We're approaching the end of the book, but I have one final exercise for you.

Draw the graphic in Figure 12.2 on a piece of paper and at the top of the two circles, write your date of birth. Then in the middle where the two circles overlap, put today's date.

That top circle, from the day you were born until today, is full of all the things that you have done in your life so far, and there is nothing you can do about any of it. It's gone. So if you are walking around like I was before I got sick, saying 'this happened to me' and 'that happened to me' and allowing it to weigh you down, you need to let it go. My doctor at the time was amazing. She made me make a list of all that stuff and take it into the garden and burn it. I am not a new-age person at all, but my goodness it was an amazing feeling to let it all go.

The bottom circle, from today's date, represents the rest of your life.

FIGURE 12.2   Future exercise

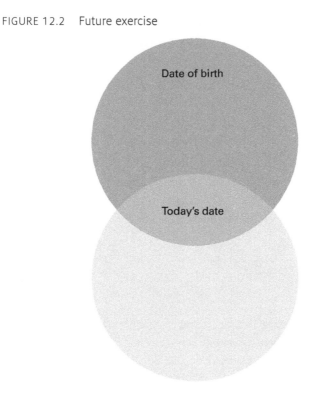

So, what are you going to do with it? Because it could be anything you want it to be.

The bottom circle brings us full circle. It reminds us of Jeff Hoffman's story about his friend John and thinking about legacy and what you want yours to be. It takes you back to that fourth quadrant of the Johari Window, which is the things you don't know about yourself and nobody else knows about you either – YET. And we're back to right at the beginning of the book when I talked about you doing things that make your heart sing and that you have fallen in love with your role and its potential all over again. My most fervent wish for you is that when you close this book, you go and do things with your life and career that make your heart sing and that you have fallen in love with your role and its potential all over again. Because if you are miserable in your work, and have no life outside it, what's the point? In the end only two things matter, the lessons and the blessings, and everything is either one or the other.

I'm going to leave you with my very favourite quote in the world, which is another one from Mark Twain. It sums up what I want to leave you with very neatly.

Twenty years from now you will be more disappointed by the things that you didn't do than by the ones you did do. So, throw off the bowlines. Sail away from the safe harbor. Catch the trade winds in your sails. Explore. Dream. Discover.

References

Cole, W (2004) Please, go away, *Time*, https://content.time.com/time/magazine/article/0,9171,709054,00.html (archived at https://perma.cc/MXP6-K6AG)

Dovico.com (nd) Time management facts and figures, https://www.dovico.com/blog/2018/03/06/time-management-facts-figures/ (archived at https://perma.cc/K7LQ-UULD)

HSE (2022) Annual work-related ill-health and injury statistics for 2021/22, https://press.hse.gov.uk/2022/11/23/hse-publishes-annual-work-related-ill-health-and-injury-statistics-for-2021-22/ (archived at https://perma.cc/M5MP-C55M)

Mazur, C (2023) 40+ worrisome workplace stress statistics [2023]: Facts, causes, and trends, Zippia, https://www.zippia.com/advice/workplace-stress-statistics/ (archived at https://perma.cc/PL2Z-HRRD)

Book club questions

- Which part of the book resonated most with you?
- Which new tip will you find most useful?
- How might you go about implementing the Global Skills Matrix at your company?
- Which suggestions do you think would be most useful to implement across your team?
- Which parts of the book did you find particularly inspiring?
- How can we help our managers to better utilize their administrative functions?
- What new systems and processes could we implement that would help to give your managers back time?
- How can we change the perception of this role?
- How can we make this a career of choice for school or college leavers?
- What three things would you like to implement or do differently after reading this book in order to position yourself as a strategic business partner?

Index

Printed in the USA
CPSIA information can be obtained
at www.ICGtesting.com
JSHW072139040923
47802JS00006B/45

9 781398 612204